RAISED BY OUR CHILDHOOD VOICES

One father's journey to raise confident, connected, compassionate boys

Darrell Brown

Edited by Christian de Quincey

DISCLAIMER PLEASE READ

Copyright© 2015 Darrell Brown | All Rights Reserved.

The people, events and stories depicted in this book are for educational purposes only and offers a representation of some of what is possible for an individual. All names have been used with permission or changed to protect the identity of the individuals in question. While every attempt has been made to verify information provided in this book, the author assumes no responsibility for any errors, inaccuracies or omissions.

The examples within this book are not intended to represent or guarantee that everyone or anyone will achieve their desired results. Each individual's success will be determined by his or her desire, dedication, effort and motivation. There are no guarantees you will achieve your desired outcome and the tools, stories and information are provided as examples only not as a guarantee you will experience the same or similar results.

First edition 2015 | Copyright 2015 by Darrell Brown

Edited by Christian de Quincey
Cover Photograph by Darrell Brown

All rights reserved. No part of this book may be reproduced, stored in a retrieval system or transmitted in any form by an electronic, mechanical, photocopying, recording means or otherwise without prior permission of the author and publisher Darrell Brown.

Discover More About The Power Of Parenting Boys at
www.darrellbrown.com.au

Self Published

ISBN-10: 978-0-9943098-0-8

Darrell Brown

103 Arnott Street

Trigg Western Australia 6029

FOREWORD

I am delighted to write a brief foreword to Darrell Brown's wide and fascinating book "Raised by Our Childhood Voices." Through our many conversations in the dazzling, raw wonderland of the outback around Uluru, I came to meet a man of real wisdom and radical commitment to spiritual transformation and the work of love in life. I was especially moved by Darrell's unabashed celebration of his love for his sons and his understanding of sacred importance of such a love, both for his own evolution and theirs, and for men in general.

There is a new masculinity emerging in our time – a grounded, confident, loving masculinity – dedicated to honouring and protecting the feminine. Darrell himself exemplifies this masculine nature and told me again and again how one of his deepest joys as a man was to foster a healthy, strong, and sensitive masculinity in his sons to equip them to be pioneers of a new way of being and doing everything in our world of crisis. I was so struck by what Darrell was saying, and the way he was saying it, that I asked him strongly to write this book.

I am so glad that I did. "Raised by Our Childhood Voices" is a fine book, moving, eloquent, packed with stories, confessions, deep and authentic spiritual information and discovery. It is both an enthralling and sometimes scaldingly honest memoir and a passionate plea to all men to uncover and live the deep, brave love of their true nature. Here's hoping, dear Darrell, that this book will be the first of many, and that its many inspiring and helpful messages will reach as large an audience as possible.

Andrew Harvey, Author of "The Hope"

DEDICATION

This book is dedicated to my wife Jules and
our two beautiful boys Cody and Taylor.

They are and always will be the reason I wake up every
morning with a smile on my face and love in my heart.

To Jules, my companion,
my guide, my lover, my best friend.

To Cody and Taylor thanks for giving me
the gift of fatherhood.

I love you eternally.

CONTENTS

Foreword 3
Dedication 5
Introduction 9

1. Looking Back 13
2. An Old Soul 21
3. A Voice from the Past 28
4. The Greatest Gift 36
5. Coming Home 48
6. Wild at Heart 52
7. Being There.. 64
8. The Treehouse... 68
9. Do You Believe? 75
10. A World Gone Mad... 82
11. Those Teenage Years 95
12. Mr. President... 105
13. A Need To Know 119
14. You Can't Teach Passion 133
15. Join Up 139
16. Lost In Space 147
17. The Science Of Compassion 157
18. The Secret To Life 169

19. The Mystic, The Elder, And The Rock 178
20. A Bigger Connection 194
21. A Parental Evolution 211
22. Reconnection 219

Afterword 223
References And Resources 227
Acknowledgments 229
About The Author, Darrell Brown 231
Continue Your Journey 235
Praise For Raised By Our Childhood Voices 237

INTRODUCTION

In our quietest moments, we softly hear the voices of our distant childhood. These whispers from the past often return to guide our journey into adulthood and, ultimately, shape us into who we become. Surely, then, the words we use as we raise our own children are powerful forces in their lives—perhaps the most potent force. Knowing this invites us to view parenting as a great responsibility—perhaps the greatest.

I am not a child psychologist. I never studied at university. In fact, I have no formal academic training at all. I am simply a father of two young boys, who, with my wife by my side, has been able to navigate through the role of parenting with a certain amount of what some might call "success." The journey certainly hasn't been without its struggles. Like everyone else, I have experienced a mix of good and bad days—some days when I thought I knew exactly what I was doing and others when I felt completely lost. Parenting, after all, is a journey that none of us is ever really prepared for.

However, from the first day our boys arrived, we bathed them in a sea of love, and that in itself has ultimately allowed us to weather any storm. Without love, you have nothing at all. Some might say there's never been a more difficult time in history to raise children. They might be right. Certainly, our technology-driven world has created a whole new set of parenting challenges that no previous generation had to contend with.

Though the basic parenting principles of the past still apply, parents today need to be much more aware of the rapidly changing environment within which we have to raise our children. Unlike for past generations, today's distractions are pervasive—in the home, on the street, in stores, on TV, on the Internet. As parents, we have slowly lost control of the external influences that now bombard our children. A tsunami of social media, television, and a constant stream of digital messages now compete with us daily for our children's attention.

In our children's lives, there are some things we can change, but other things we simply can't. In this book, I will focus more on the things we can.

I want to begin with an invitation. I ask you to open up to the idea that, as a parent, you are without doubt the most powerful influence on your child's life. You are, indeed, their best bet. With this influence comes great responsibility. But then, who would have it any other way? Becoming a parent was the greatest challenge of my life, and one I looked forward to immensely. The opportunity to be a father is, after all, the greatest gift ever bestowed upon a man. Aiming to be a great father drove every decision I made and took up every spare minute. But my commitment gave me the strength I needed at every step, to face any challenge. To be my boys' best bet would require nothing less.

I made being a great father my number one priority. Hardly a day went by when I wasn't totally immersed in my boys' lives. I knew that every day they grew older was a day I could never get back. I certainly didn't want any regrets and, I'm happy to say, I have very few.

In order to spend time with my boys, many pastimes and hobbies I had before fatherhood took a back seat—and I was more than happy to make the trade. My golf, scuba diving, and drinks with my mates were now less of a priority. In this transition I never felt happier or more alive. I knew that I was doing the most important thing imaginable with my time.

I am writing this book based on my own experience as a father. However, I also openly acknowledge that without the wonderful and reliable support and contribution from my wife, Jules, I could never have become the father I am. Her constant words of wisdom have always kept me on track when I ventured off course. I also want to be clear that throughout this book I speak more directly about raising *boys* and not girls. To be authentic, I can only write about what I know and have experienced. However, I believe that any parenting wisdom you may find in this book can be universal in its application—for boys and girls. The unconditional love I feel as a father of two boys goes beyond gender. Love transcends any such differences.

This book tells a two-part story. The first part reflects on the journey of my boyhood, growing up with my father, and the effect that had on my life. In the second part, I describe my own experience as a father and how I applied what I learned to our two boys. I have found in my own life that the greatest way to prepare for parenthood was to begin by looking backwards.

After all, most of the beliefs we carry with us into the role of parenting we picked up as children. For some of us, childhood was a wholesome experience. For many others, however, we find that a lot of things didn't "work." Part of growing into a well-adjusted adult capable of raising loving children comes from our ability to examine our lives and, hopefully, make the necessary adjustments. The greatest challenge to parenting comes from unexamined beliefs that still run our lives at the unconscious level.

This book tells the stories, the trials and tribulations, of my own life—and how those experiences shaped the way I raised our two boys. As you will see, I am certainly not the perfect father; I have no idea what that would even look like. But I have achieved many things with my boys that appear to have worked, and I have given much thought to why that is. There are also many times in this book when I refer directly to the educational aspects of parenting that I have studied and learnt along the way. You'll see that the content sometimes changes between the narrative of my own life and the theory behind the choices I made.

I hope that somewhere within these pages you will be inspired to take some of the ideas that have worked for me and apply them to your own life as a parent. If I can meet you somewhere within these pages, perhaps together we can raise children who will make a lasting contribution to a better world. More importantly, I hope that *your* experience as a parent will bring you as much love, joy, and wonder as raising our two boys has for Jules and me.

As we begin this journey, let's be guided by the words of that great Sufi poet—Rumi:

"Out beyond the boundaries of right and wrong, there is a field, and I shall meet you there."

1

LOOKING BACK

Growing up as a young boy wasn't easy. My parents moved to Australia from the U.K. in 1969 and, as "ten pound poms," we arrived by ship in the port of Fremantle, Western Australia. I was five years old, the youngest of three children. My sister was a year older than me, and my brother five years older than her. We had been in Australia less than a year when my parents separated. I never saw it coming, and their break-up came as a complete shock. At five, I guess there's "your world" and then there's the harsh reality of life. When both worlds collide, it takes a while to find solid ground again.

To this day, I'm still not exactly sure what happened. All I remember is that I didn't see my mum again for another fifteen years.

We had many ups and downs. My dad did his best to raise the three of us. Working long hours and trying to pay the bills, he wasn't around as much as we would have liked. The time I did get with my dad was always precious. Although things were tough, I remember that period as perhaps the happiest of my childhood. We never had much money, but at least our home environment was peaceful and caring—which, as I was later to find out, is a vital ingredient for the mental wellbeing of a young boy. In Dad's absence, my older brother did well to look after my sister and me, which probably robbed him a lot of his own childhood. I guess that's often the burden of being the oldest sibling.

I don't think I have ever been as close to my dad as I was then. When I want fond memories of my father, I often go back to those years. As young children, we always think the life we live will never change. It is all one encompassing "now." But I discovered that definitely was not the case.

Three or so years later, my father got engaged again. He had met a shy but warm lady, the daughter of a senator. Although my memory of her from that time is vague, I recall she was very caring and I grew fond of her. She began to fill the role of a nurturing mother—something that all small boys need. Trying to plug a void left by my mum, I longed for someone to cuddle and be close to.

A wedding day was set and my thoughts of being a family again were starting to take shape. However just days before the wedding, my dad's fiancé went missing.

The police put out a missing person's bulletin and started searching for her. Four days later, they found her—parked in a national forest with a hose running from the exhaust pipe into the window of the car. She had taken her own life.

As an eight-year old boy, I found it hard to understand the adult world. All I knew was that my world was thrown into confusion once again. I struggled to make sense of it all. My father never spoke much about what happened. Not for the first time, my siblings and I were left to try to figure things out for ourselves. I guess Dad was trying to do the same. Losing a mum once is hard enough, but a second time can really mess with your mind. I never blamed my dad for either of those events. If anything, they brought us closer. I promised him that when I grew up, I would never leave him—a promise that would eventually challenge me in my adult years.

As children, we create beliefs about the world based on our experiences. Having lost two "mums" by age eight, I guess I could have been forgiven for believing I wasn't worthy of a woman's love. We make up stories as children, trying to make sense of the world. Feeling our survival depends on it, we make decisions and form beliefs about how the world is. Those stories might give us some comfort while we are kids, but when we carry them over into our adult years, they can often restrict our growth.

The greatest challenge of growing into a fully functioning adult comes from our ability to become aware of our unexamined childhood beliefs. We create these beliefs based on the meaning we gave to our experiences. Typically, bad experiences lead to negative stories, good ones to positive stories. But because we come to believe them, our stories become reality for us—in both supportive and dysfunctional ways. Our beliefs become our identity. In any case, at age eight, the pain of being hurt again felt like too much for me to handle. It seemed safer to create the belief, "I'm just not worthy."

A couple of years later, my father entered into what was to become his third and final relationship. He married a woman with two boys from a previous marriage. Unlike the warm feelings I had for his previous fiancée, I never felt any kind of connection to my "new mum." Strangers right from the start, we never got any closer. If anything, with each passing year, we drifted farther apart. Although deep down I longed for a loving relationship, my stepmother was not the type of person who could fill that void. Probably still struggling with her own childhood issues, she never appeared willing or even capable of creating a loving bond. She was resentful of the close relationship I had with my father and did everything she could to tear us apart. Not only me; she resented anyone who got in the way, including my brother and sister. Over the years, I saw many of Dad's friends drift away. The only people who came into our lives were those she selected.

Dad worked long hours, and we were often left to fend for ourselves. The peaceful, caring home I had been used to morphed into an uneasy, sometimes even hostile, environment. Alcohol became part of the evening ritual. I would sit and watch as my stepmother smoked cigarette after cigarette while consuming glasses of wine. Dad hadn't been much of a drinker, so seeing someone drink to the point of passing out on the kitchen floor unnerved me.

When Dad finally got home from work, it grew increasingly difficult to have any one-on-one time. Sometimes he would take the dog for a late-night walk and I would try to sneak out the back door without being spotted. I wanted to catch up with him and stroll along side by side. Unfortunately, my stepmom placed herself right outside my bedroom door, and blocked my "great escapes."

"Leave him alone!" she would snap. "He doesn't need you bugging him while he walks the dog."

As a young boy I was small for my age. I clearly remember looking at each year's class photo and being half the size of most boys in my class. Looking young for your age is fine as an adult but as a boy it can sometimes work against you. Coming home from school wasn't always a happy experience and often we weren't allowed anything to eat until dinnertime...two hours away! On one particular afternoon, I couldn't help myself, so I got on my bike and rode to the local shopping centre. With an empty stomach, and without any money, I walked into a large convenience store, opened a small packet of Mars bars, and helped myself to one. Thinking no one had seen me, I walked out. A hand grabbed my shoulder. A plain-clothes security woman took me to a small room at the back of the shop and proceeded to take my details. At first, thinking I was about eleven, she was simply going to give me a warning. But when she discovered I was fourteen, she informed me she was required to call the police.

Terrified, I begged her not to, but to no avail. Two uniformed police officers arrived and marched me through the store. People stood and stared at me, and I wondered what they must have been thinking. My whole body felt numb even as a tsunami of emotions washed through me—fear, anxiety, embarrassment, and...always back to fear. When we finally reached the front of the store, my heart sunk even further. Right there by the curb, in broad daylight, a police paddy wagon waited to take me...where? Home? Prison? For one small Mars bar?

One of the police officers was female, so I looked to her and asked if there was any chance I go in the front of the vehicle. At my young age, the thought of being locked in the back of the police wagon was too terrible to imagine. Against the better judgment of the male officer, they agreed to let me sit up front. In the midst of all the darkness, I felt I had found an ally.

When scared, it's easy to lose your perspective on life—especially as children. At that moment, I felt my entire world caving in on me. As they drove me home, a new rush of anxiety swept over me. I'd surely be in fearsome trouble. As we pulled into the driveway, I could see that Dad wasn't home yet. My stepmother opened the door, and my sorry plight must have made her year. She immediately sent me to my room, and I thought that that was the end of it. But more drama was unfolding—even without my presence.

Twenty-four hours earlier, as I was walking home from school, I had found an old basketball at the end of my street. No one else was around, so I picked it up. I noticed some faded letters on the ball, identifying my high school. I playfully bounced the ball home. Big mistake!

After about half an hour, I was summoned from my bedroom to the lounge. The police were still there, which surprised me.

"Your mum tells us you've been stealing from the high school!" the male officer said. From then on, everything became a blur of words and faces. Did she really tell the police that I stole an old basketball from the school? Who would even want the old thing?

Looking back, I see that as a defining moment in my life. I completely lost the last trace of trust in someone who was meant to care for me. I knew she didn't like me; I just never realised how much. The two officers told me I would have to appear in front of some juvenile offender's panel, and that there may be further punishment. The police left, and I was exiled back to my room.

What would I say to Dad when he got home? I knew my stepmother would get to him first, but I thought for sure he would at least listen to my side of the story once he calmed down. Who knows, maybe he would give me some kind words of comfort or advice. Perhaps a story from his own past, one of his own misadventures? Most of all, though, I wanted him to give me a hug. I was just a boy and I was scared. What I really needed was to feel loved.

When Dad finally came home, I tried as hard as I could to hear the conversation down the hall. She immediately whisked him straight into their bedroom, and shut the door. All I could do was wait.

After what seemed a small eternity, my bedroom door opened.

"Your father wants to see you in our bedroom!" she said with a smile. I hesitantly entered Dad's bedroom, looking for that hug. He met me holding his belt. I don't remember feeling the second and third hit, but I clearly remember counting them. I guess no discussion was needed.

As the years went on, I began to rely more and more on myself for anything I needed. I guess I stopped thinking of Dad as my hero. Though I still loved him, I felt sad at the distance growing between us. I remember sometimes trying to fall asleep at night hearing my stepmother refer to me as "that little c*nt!" One night, a thought finally dawned on me with a new sense of loss. Even if what she was saying about me happened to be true...why didn't he remind her of my name? *I have a name!* I thought to myself. *I have a name.*

I think at a subconscious level I lost some respect for my father. Deep down, I knew he still loved me, but the person I get angry; the other is to simply get curious. The problem with getting angry is that it cuts off the opportunity for understanding. I find life's richness comes from trying to understand why people do the things they do rather than judge them for it. This concept is easy to write in a book, but managing our emotions constantly challenges the best of us in our daily lives.

It had been fifteen years since I had seen my mum. As it turned out, she was now living in Australia. She had returned from South Africa where she had remarried and had another son—my two-year-old half-brother, Thomas. Though now living in the same country, my mum was still about a thousand kilometres away in Darwin, a remote capital city at the top end of northern Australia.

A former international model, mum had now turned her attention to working with the local indigenous communities. Someone had obviously noticed her various qualities and nominated her for the "Mrs. Australia competition." She won Mrs. Northern Territory, and went on to become the first woman from the NT to win Mrs. Australia. As part of her official duties, she was to tour Australia from state to state, helping to raise money for charities and speaking out on various women's issues.

"I'm coming to Perth next month!" she explained. "I would love to meet up with you and your sister."

I must have hesitated, because she continued, "I would rather explain things to you in person than over the phone."

I immediately agreed to meet with her. My head started to fill with questions that hadn't been with me since childhood: How could a mother leave her children? *Why* would a mother leave her children? Although Dad had given me various reasons, and had done his best to raise the three us, I was desperate to hear my mother's side of the story.

had loved—my protector, my hero—was now gone. The loving father I once knew was becoming a distant memory.

Now a father myself, I sometimes think back to that young boy who still lives inside me. I think of the words I would love to have said to him in his hours of need. I wish I could have been there to give him a hug and tell him everything was going to be okay. I can sometimes feel the sadness that "he" must have felt. I wish I could have been there for him.

I guess in some ways, now I can.

2

AN OLD SOUL

They say an "old soul" is someone who has been here before. I left home at seventeen, and for some reason that was exactly how I felt. Something about my life already seemed familiar. Not that I ever had any flashbacks to a previous life; more like wisdom beyond my years. I felt a connection to something much bigger than me. A voice inside told me things were going to be okay. That "inner voice" could have been my deep unconscious mind, an intuition, my old soul, or perhaps even a whisper from the divine. Call it what you will, but I think sometimes we have to search for strength from a place deeper inside ourselves.

In my final year of high school, I completely bombed out. I got the lowest TAE (Tertiary Admittance Examination) score among my friends, and there were some pretty dumb kids at my high school! I had enjoyed school very much because it meant I wasn't at home. Academically, however, the only subjects that really interested me were film and TV. Video making sounded exciting, and from what I had heard, it was one of the easiest courses to get into at university.

Despite my crappy exam results, I thought they would accept me at college—if for my enthusiasm alone. After all, I had completed Year 12 and I did get *some* sort of score. At that time, only two universities existed in town, and both rejected my application. They suggested I re-sit Year 12 and try again the following year—an option I wasn't the least bit interested in.

I grew up with a kind of naive optimism about life—perhaps because I was an old soul? Not one to be easily stopped, I decided to look for a way into the TV industry. A few weeks later, my brother called to find out if I was still interested in a career in film and TV. He told me about a flyer he had seen at teacher's college asking for "extras" to be in a crowd scene for a local TV series. He said they were paying ten dollars for the day and lunch was supplied. It wasn't much, but I saw it as a good sign. The next day, I took two buses to get close to the location, followed by a two-kilometer walk. As I stood in the crowd all day, all I could think about was being on the other side of the camera. It looked exciting and everyone seemed to be having such a great time—a land of make believe where nothing was real. It looked like fun. In an odd kind of way, it also looked like family.

When the crowd dispersed at the end of the shoot, I remained a lone figure on my side of the rope. I walked over to where the cameraman was still packing up—a polite English gentleman by the name of Ian Pugsley. I'll never forget what I said next.

"Is this a job?" I asked.

He paused, and gave me a strange look. But I seriously wanted to know. Back then, the only career options I was told about at school were plumber, bank teller, engineer —that type of thing. No one ever told me I could be a cinematographer and get paid to fly around the world making movies.

"Yes, I guess this is a job of sorts," he replied.

"Great," I said, "How do I get a job?"

"There are no jobs," he replied. Although that wasn't the answer I was hoping for, it was perfectly correct. No one ever advertised in the local paper for a cameraman to travel the world shooting wonderful images. Jobs like that came from being "in the know." Besides having the basic skills and experience, of course, good connections made all the difference. I stood there for a second, and then asked the only other question I could think of.

"Where are you going to be tomorrow?"

Success in life often comes not by getting the right answer, but by asking the right questions.

"We are here again tomorrow."

"Great, I'll see you then!" I meant it. I now had a mission.

The next morning, I woke up early and caught the first bus into town; jumped on a second bus out to Fremantle, and again walked two clicks to the shoot location. I didn't have any video skills or experience to offer, but I could lift heavy things. I played to my strengths, and looked around for the "gaffer"—the guy in charge of hauling and setting up the lighting equipment.

I was introduced to Ray Thomas, a wiry old guy who looked after the lighting, and seemed to be doing the most of the heavy lifting. I immediately attached myself to Ray. For some reason, he took a shining to me. Warren Buffett once said, "You're lucky in life if you pick the right heroes." I know exactly what he meant. Every boy needs a hero. For most boys, it's their dad. But for some, it doesn't turn out that way, and the journey can be tough. Without a hero for guidance, it's easy to become disillusioned with life.

I guess that's what Warren Buffett was saying: We need strong role models at different stages of our lives to guide us to the next part of our journey. But we also need to be smart enough to recognise our heroes along the way. Actually, maybe it's not about being smart enough, but more about being open to receiving their support. When you've been let down so many times, so early in life, sometimes it's hard to build that trust.

Ray soon became one of my heroes and it didn't take long for him to spot one of my natural abilities, something that would prove very useful in the hustle and bustle of the film business: I could run fast! Ray soon had me racing back and forth to the lighting truck to get some piece of gear or another.

"Hey Darrell! Grab me a C stand, and a Red Head, plus a cutter and a roll of 85. Now get me a 2k Blondie, a sand bag, and a piece of polly!"

I quickly got to know every bit of gear in the truck and watched Ray as he helped the director of photography to light each scene. My enthusiasm on set didn't go unnoticed, and I quickly got to know the guys in the camera department. They took me under their wing and often let me help set up the camera and look through the lens. They would get me to frame shots and then explain why a particular angle was better than others.

Meal breaks were catered. I ate well, and, hungry for knowledge, I used the time to ask questions of everyone on the crew. Of course that's not how I had been in school, where there's generally no context for the information. Most of what you learn in school doesn't make sense because it doesn't fit into your life. This new knowledge I was gaining now served a purpose.

As the weeks rolled on, I worked fourteen-to-sixteen-hour days, six days a week. All for absolutely no pay! The thought of money hadn't really crossed my mind. Some of my friends said I was crazy to work for free, and that they could get me a well-paid job on a building site anytime I wanted it. My response was always the same: "I don't want a job, thanks...I'm going to be a cameraman."

After about three months, the assistant director approached me, looking worried.

"Hey Darrell, the production manager wants to see you right away!" he yelled.

My heart sank. I had heard lots of things about the production manager and none of them were good. Although we had never met, I knew where her office was and immediately made the long walk to her door. I stood in the doorway, but she kept writing, her head down.

"Did you want to see me?" I asked.

Without lifting her head she replied, "Yes. It appears we've got a problem."

"What's the problem?" I asked.

"You. You're the problem."

I swallowed hard. "Why am I a problem?"

"Because you won't go away...and that means you're an insurance risk." My heart sank even more. I could see my wonderful career in cinematography coming to a short and abrupt close.

She looked straight at me. "That means we have to give you a job." I could hardly believe my ears. She continued, "As of

Monday, you will join the crew as a best boy (gaffer's assistant). You start on $132.00 per week. Congratulations, and welcome aboard!" Her face broke into a smile.

The job lasted for another three months, and in that time I made enough contacts and got enough experience to set me up for the rest of my life. My initial salary of $132.00 was more money than I had ever seen before. I saved enough to buy my first car. Now I had freedom, aligned with my purpose and my passion. When I had first arrived on set six months previously, I was told there weren't any jobs. Instead of accepting that and walking away, I persisted, and followed my heart's desire. Or maybe it was my soul's desire. Had I not done so, my life would have been very different today.

When you refuse to take no for an answer and slowly continue to move toward your dreams, anything becomes possible. Learning to ask the right questions along the way makes all the difference. When you tell the world, "I'll do it or die," remember that the universe doesn't want you to die. As you commit, doors will open up to new opportunities. Each of us possesses an inner energy that connects us to unseen universal forces, and I believe the deepest part of us constantly dialogues with the universe. Whatever we "put out," the universe responds accordingly.

When I heard "there aren't any jobs," I simply let it wash right over me because it wasn't part of the future I had planned for myself. The universe tests us, early on, to see how committed we are. When I heard "no jobs available," I took it as a sign that I needed to ask better questions. Without passion and a strong desire to follow your dreams, you will give up at the first closed door.

Growing up in a dysfunctional home environment worked for me and against me. In some respects, it made me realise early on that if I was going to get anywhere in life, it would be up to me. My challenging early years made me self-driven and determined to succeed. I also felt grateful toward anyone who showed me support and kindness—something that I had sometimes missed in my childhood, and craved in my early adult years.

On the downside, I would often doubt myself. Although I had a strong drive to succeed, I frequently questioned my ability to make it happen. As adults, it's not always easy to escape our childhood voices—those that block us as well as those that guide us.

Being told, year after year, that you are worthless can take its toll. Even after all these years, my childhood voices—both positive and negative—remain with me today. My task is to *learn to listen* to these voices, know which to trust and which to ignore, and listen to the voices that support me.

Check in with your soul from time to time. Reaffirm what you know to be your purpose and passion in life. Remember: *The universe always responds.* It is *always* listening. Our job is to ask the right questions, to express our true desires, and to make the necessary commitments—and, of course, to listen for the inevitable feedback.

3

A VOICE FROM THE PAST

Just short of my twentieth birthday, I got the phone call.

"Darrell darling, is that you?"

She had left when I was only five years old, and I had not seen or heard from her since. I had no recollection of my mother's voice. At the time, **no one** in my life referred to me as "Darrell darling."

"Who's this?" I asked, curiously.

"It's me. Your mum."

All of us can think back to specific moments that changed our lives. Having just joined the biggest TV production house in Australia, I was sharply focused on my *future*. Now this call hit me like a train, reverberating from the deepest part of my past.

"Mum! Is that you?" I was lost for words.

Years later as a father I would often tell my boys that when someone hurts you, you have two ways to respond. The first is to

I arranged to meet her at the hotel in the city where she was staying. My sister, came with me. I got out of the elevator and walked along the corridor, searching for the room number. My older brother was away at the time, so only two of us now stood anxiously outside her hotel room.

Thirty years later, I don't recall a lot of the conversation. We tend to remember the feeling of an encounter long after we have forgotten the words. Mum was careful to find out about who we were now rather than tell us why she had left. Rather than bring back bad memories of her leaving, she wanted to find out as much as she could about those missing fifteen years.

She longed to be a bigger part of our lives, and I could see how much the pain of missing all those early years with her children had taken its toll. She said she had tried to write us letters and desperately wanted to see us when we were young. Given the environment at home at the time, I can understand why a lot of those messages didn't get through.

Mum and dad had strikingly different stories about why she left. She told of a very unhappy time and a volatile marriage. However, because my time with Dad in those early years had been happy, I struggled to make sense of what she said. Years later, I asked Dad if any of what Mum had said was true, and I gave examples of specific stories she had told us. None of it resonated with him. In fact, comparing both stories about why they separated, it seemed that they had lived two completely different lives. How could two people be married and have completely different stories of what actually transpired? Was one lying and the other telling the truth? In the end, I made peace with the idea that I would never really know.

We all make decisions in life that we later regret. In order to deal with this, we often make up stories that justify our actions. It then becomes much easier to live with the story than to deal with the pain. Perhaps none of what they told me was completely accurate; maybe the truth was somewhere in the middle. I certainly wasn't looking to blame either parent; I was simply doing what anyone in my situation would do: looking for understanding about my childhood.

From that time onward, I saw my mother at regular intervals. It took time to get to know her again, and because of my stepmother, we decided to keep our relationship quiet to avoid any trouble. However, as I began to grow into a young man, I battled with the secrecy. It didn't feel right that, as adults, we couldn't be more honest with each other about our relationships.

Although both my sister and older brother also slowly rebuilt their relationships with Mum, neither felt comfortable inviting her to their weddings. Instead, they met in secret before or after the event. When I asked them about that, they both told me it was to keep the peace. I understood, and certainly didn't judge them for their decision.

Jules and I met when I was 24, but didn't marry until I turned 30. We drew up a list of people we wanted at our wedding, including friends and family from interstate and overseas. We invited people who were in our hearts and with whom we had shared many wonderful times. Mum was on the list too. In my heart, I had always known we would invite her.

I called Dad to let him know Mum would be coming. I didn't realise how nervous I would be until I actually picked up the phone to dial. Besides being taken aback by the fact that Mum and I were even in touch, Dad totally refused to be in the same room with her. He obviously felt betrayed, and he let me know, "Well Darrell, if she's coming to the wedding, then I won't be there." I could hear the disappointment in his voice.

My brother and sister both tried to convince me to change my mind.

"Maybe you should tell Mum you will see her afterwards. You can't not have Dad at the wedding. It will cause way too much trouble." They wanted to keep the peace and I couldn't blame them.

When Jules asked me what I would do, I said I would call Dad again and try to straighten things out. I wanted him to know I wasn't angry; I just needed him to try and understand the reasons behind my decision. Although the youngest in the family, I felt that it was up to me to try to resolve our differences. Surely we could all find a way to forgive and move on in our lives. Sometimes life isn't always about keeping the peace; it's more about being true to yourself.

Jules totally got where I was coming from. Never for a moment did she doubt my decision. She knew it came from my heart and that I had no intention of causing trouble. She understood me, and that's what I love about her. All I wanted was give people the opportunity to grow, forgive, and make peace with their past. Of course, you can never guarantee that others will embrace that moment on offer; you can only create the opportunity for it to happen.

Sometimes by "keepings things a secret," we inadvertently conspire to prevent people from facing their past. We take away the opportunity to grow, forgive, and move on. It's never an easy conversation to begin and often takes great courage. For many people, the pain of being hurt is still too strong. Without sufficient psychological or emotional resources to deal with something in their past, it's a subject they simply avoid. And that's understandable.

I've heard it said that the greatest gift you can ever give yourself is to forgive those who hurt you the most. It doesn't mean you have to welcome them back into your life with open arms. It just means you release the anger and pain from your own life. By "not wanting to cause trouble," perhaps we take away the opportunity for others to do just that.

So I picked up the phone, even more nervous than the first time. "Hi, Dad. It's me," I started the conversation. "I understand you're disappointed that I invited Mum to our wedding. But I want you to know something. When you and Mum broke up I know it must have been a very difficult time for you both. I have never forgotten that you did everything you could to look after us and raise us as best you could. But you also raised me to stand up for what I believe in and be true to myself and that's what I am doing now." I paused to catch my breath.

"Dad, I want you to know that if you choose not to come to my wedding, I won't love you any less. I will be desperately disappointed you're not there, but I will understand your reasons for doing so. Jules and I invited everyone to our wedding who means something to us, and that includes both you and Mum."

"Darrell, if she comes your wedding, I won't be there, so you need to decide." His position remained unchanged.

"Dad, you're *both* invited to my wedding—that is my decision. Whether you come or not is now up to you."

Over the following weeks, my brother and sister both tried to get me to change my mind, but I felt confident that Dad will be there and that everything would be fine. This I knew in my heart. As the wedding day approached, Dad finally relented. He called to say he was coming, but wasn't happy about my decision. I told him how happy we were and that I loved him dearly.

The day before the wedding, Mum came to see me. She thought I had shown great courage to follow through and be true to myself. She was happy to be sitting at a small table at the rear of the room with her husband, and my half brother. She sat quietly at the back of the church and didn't draw any attention to herself. Finally, she got to see one of her children get married—and for that she was truly grateful.

At some point, I think each of us has to decide if we want to continue to pass down to our children the things that didn't work in our own family. If I had kept secret my relationship with Mum, then where to from there? Was I simply to hand this mess along to my boys?

"Shhh, when Grandad comes over, don't tell him you have been seeing Grandma!" I don't think so. Sometimes we have to be the ones that stand up in our lineage and say, "This ends with me! No more will I continue to contribute to the wounds of our past." The moment you begin to draw a line in the sand that says "never gain," you immediately begin to heal the wounds of so many that have gone before you.

To this day, my wedding remains the only time that our entire family has been in the same room. As the years have passed, my relationship with my mum has blossomed, while the connection with my father seems to have drifted—not because of the things that happened in the past, but simply because of how they continue show up in my life now. I really don't think our role is to try to change people; rather, it's to provide them with the opportunity to do so. Having the wisdom to know how to do this with love rather than judgment is, perhaps, our greatest challenge.

4

THE GREATEST GIFT

For most people my age, the morning of October 22, 1999, was probably just another day at the office, but I had been preparing for this special day my whole life. I woke up alone in an empty house, feeling incredible excitement. I hadn't gotten much sleep. How could I? By the time this day was over, I would never see life the same way again. Fortunately, I was well prepared. Driving to the hospital, I began thinking about how it all started four long years before...

* * *

As a freelance cameraman, my life often took me to faraway places. It wasn't unusual for me to arrive home from a trip to Africa only to be back on a plane the following week to Indonesia, Vietnam, or the Philippines. At the age of thirty I married Jules', the love of my life. Six years earlier, my best friend had married her sister. As luck would have it, we were both thrown together in the wedding party. I immediately fell in love with her beautiful smile, cheeky sense of humour and genuine care for other people. While her sister and my best friend were still on their honeymoon Jules and I had already started dating.

Jules, was used to me being away for work. She had lived at home with her parents her whole life; however, now that we were married, although working full time my being away meant she often spent time on her own. To help things out, we decided it was time to hear the pitter patter of little feet. Yep, that's right…we got a puppy. We both loved animals and wanted a dog that would be great with children. Kids were also in the bigger picture and this seemed like good preparation. We settled on a golden retriever. After locating a breeder in the local paper, we arrived at the breeder's house to find only one puppy left out of a litter of nine. It was love at first sight. Six-week-old "Molly" came home in a red bucket. Fourteen years later, she sits at my side as I write these words. Jules calls her "our firstborn." I feel the same way.

A six-week-old puppy will teach you much about yourself. Puppies require patience, responsibility, and unconditional love. It takes a lot of effort to train and care for them. As they grow, however, the rewards are many. Someone once said that taking care of the outside of a dog is good for the inside of a human.

When Molly was still a pup, I used to put my hand in her meal while she ate. Of course, the food was hers, but I wanted her to know that in this house we share everything. I did the same with her bones. Eventually, she stopped growling at the interruption; she simply stopped eating until I removed my hand.

Years later, when the boys were born, we didn't have to worry about them getting close to her while she ate or chewed on a bone. If the boys ever crawled over to her while she ate, she simply got up and walked away. The message had gotten through: we share everything. And she always got her bone back.

Molly had a blessed life. We walked her nearly every day and she often slept on the couch with Jules while I was away. Molly received plenty of love and attention, and was treated as part of the family. We always honoured and respected her. During the day and sometimes at night, she slept outside in the front courtyard where she could peer at the world passing by through the gate bars.

One night when she was about five, I forgot to close the gate while coming in from a hectic day at work. In the morning, I woke and to my horror, I realised Molly wasn't there. I had left the gate ajar and I couldn't see her from my bedroom window. I rushed outside nearing panic. What if she had been run over by a car? Or taken by a passer-by? As I got closer to the gate, I saw her—sitting next to the letterbox, still guarding the house. She had been there all night. From that day on, we never needed to close the gate again. Some people ask us why she doesn't run away. My response is always the same: Where is she going to go?

I realised something special that day: If you make your home environment the most enjoyable, loving experience possible for those who live there, they will never leave you.

I don't remember the exact day Jules rang me from work sounding upset. Things had been building up for some time. Working for an insurance company can be soul destroying at the best of times. But for someone as sensitive to life as she is, it had started to drain her. All she really wanted to do was be a mum. She loved kids and kids loved her. She rang to ask me an important question.

She said she hated her job and wanted to quit. Though I knew she didn't like her work, I guess I never realised how much she struggled at that job. She told me she didn't want to stay another day. I think my response shocked her a little. I suggested that she leave straight away. As a freelance cameraman, I loved my job. I never even thought of it as a job. It was more of a lifestyle. I got to travel the world and meet new and interesting people every day. I could never understand why people spent their whole life doing something they didn't like. In the same way, I couldn't understand why people remained married to someone they didn't love.

I was fortunate to have both bases covered. I told Jules that whatever she decided to do, she had my full support. She arrived home from work that night, and she never went back. Over the next few months, we talked about having a family of our own. Though now working again her thoughts were more focused on becoming a mum. A young and healthy couple, we were quite relaxed about the possibility of falling pregnant right away. Eager, in fact.

We had started off thrilled about the idea of having children. Bringing home a newborn baby and starting a family was at the top of our "bucket list." Unfortunately, life doesn't always go according to plan. We started trying right away, however, as weeks rolled into months and months into years the excitement soon turned to disappointment. Disappointment turned into frustration, frustration to anger, and then finally depression. We went through it all.

Someone once said to me, "If you want to make God laugh, tell her your plans." Well, God must have had a real chuckle at our expense. The words "relaxed" and "falling pregnant" slowly drifted apart and didn't meet up again until five years later. After a couple of failed attempts at conception, Jules began her search into the wonderful world of fertility support. It's amazing just how many people have an opinion about how to become pregnant.

"Eat this, drink that, stand on your head. Take three of these twice a day. Play this song and wear these...but only on a full moon." Oh, and what the hell is a turkey baster?

Eventually, we found our way to a Chinese herbalist. Dr Chum owned a little corner shop on the outskirts of town. He was a soft-spoken, unassuming man who suggested we try some special herbs that help women with fertility. Both of us had gone through all the usual medical checks and had been told no biological reason prevented us from having children.

Dr Chum gave us root clippings and various herbs to cut up and use to make tea. At this point, we were ready to try anything. The tea tasted terrible, but Jules drank it nonetheless. We continued to make regular visits to the wise man from the East, but with little success.

As the months slowly passed, our hopes waned as the situation deteriorated. We were introduced to a medical procedure called IUIs (intrauterine insemination). Not an overly intrusive procedure, but invasive nevertheless.

It's funny how quickly trying to get pregnant can turn from a loving, intimate experience into a no-holds-barred clinical process. The romance and spontaneity quickly fade away when you're handed a timetable with a list of appointment times indicating where your services will be required.

These were difficult times for Jules. The idea of never actually becoming a mum had never before entered her mind.

It was a given that we'd have a family. Nature had provided her with all the necessary equipment, so it was easy for her to start blaming herself.

Walking into the waiting room of the IVF Medical Centre was sobering. Having exhausted all other possibilities over the years, we were finally left with what seemed our last hope for a baby. In our research over the previous months, we had heard many stories about couples who had gone down the IVF path. It seemed only two possible outcomes remained: the euphoria of becoming parents, or the pain of never having a family of our own.

After all, getting pregnant either happens or it doesn't. You can't get *nearly* pregnant. There's no middle ground. It seemed so unfair: either winners or losers in the fertility lottery, leading to immense joy or total desperation. The outcome seemed beyond our control, in God's hands.

Looking around the waiting room that morning, I could sense desperation on the faces of the women as they pretended to read the gossip magazines clutched tightly in their hands. We were the new couple. It was our first time, and they all knew it. Some of the women knew this room very well. It had been their life for the past six years, some even longer. That's what IVF does. It consumes your life. It takes over everything. It can destroy marriages and sometimes does. If you ever want to test your relationship to see what it is made of, try an IVF program.

"Now, you both understand that even with IVF, there are no guarantees you'll fall pregnant," the nurse made clear. I looked at Jules. That's not what she wanted to hear. She wanted guarantees and plenty of them! Not getting pregnant was not an option. "On the other hand, of course," the nurse continued, "with this kind of procedure there's also a risk of multiple pregnancies."

Hearing this, Jules' eyes lit up. I knew what she was thinking. *Yes! Yes! Twins!* When women get to this point, even the idea of quintuplets is completely acceptable—anything but the deep prolonged pain of a life without children.

Naturally, we took the dive into the unpredictable and extremely anxious world of IVF. Romance took a backseat to clinical procedures, timetables, and frequent visits to the local depository. Nothing adds more to an already-busy schedule than a quick stop at the clinic to unload a sample of potential swimmers. A tap on the door, an old "adult" magazine thrust in one hand to help get things going, and a small jar with your name on it in your other. I soon got used to the idea that I was now merely a pawn in a game of, "Let's get pregnant."

Little did I realise the worst was yet to come.

The life of a freelance cameraman involves dangerous adventures. Hanging out of helicopters, diving into shark tanks, and jumping out of airplanes—I had done them all and survived. But one thing scared me more then all those put together, something I had a phobia about since I was a small boy: *needles!*

At the start of each cycle, Jules had to be injected with a substance vital for providing a fertile environment for eggs. Although I didn't understand the biochemistry, to this point I had always agreed and simply did what I was told. For IVF, Jules had two options: either she got up each morning and drove to the doctor's surgery, to sit in the waiting room until he was available to administer the needle … or we had to do it ourselves. I had no problem with the first option, but it was out of the question for Jules. The thought of venturing down to the surgery each day was too much to bear. In the end, we agreed to handle things ourselves.

The memories of those extremely stressful mornings are still very clear. My first duty was to carefully break open the first vial containing the serum. Once in the head of the needle, I would then have to change the needle itself to one that would penetrate the skin. The responsibility of getting this right and not breaking the glass was immense. As I entered the bedroom, I would find Jules anxiously waiting. I had only one go at getting it right. The needle had to pierce the skin of a small area just to the left of the upper part of her buttocks. Too far to the left or right would not work at all and would also be extremely painful. The nurses at Pivet had given me some spare needles to practice on an orange. I had no problem there, but this was my wife and we both hated needles.

That first morning, summoning all my courage, I took aim and shot the needle right into its mark. I'm not sure who screamed louder, but the job wasn't over yet. I slowly had to empty the contents of the needle into her rump and as I did, her pain increased. I couldn't help thinking how vastly more enjoyable the process would have been if nature had simply taken its course.

After that painful episode, I had nothing more to do but wait.

Even if I wanted to, I could do nothing more than cheer from the sidelines. We were told to relax, and let God do the rest. Easy for the doctor and nurses to say. But I took their advice and immersed myself in my work as a cameraman. For Jules, it was a different story. She had given up work to focus on having children. It meant so much to her to be a mum and now it consumed her life.

A big cross on the calendar each month signalled the day the pregnancy test results were due. Jules always refused to take the call. Therefore, the news of any outcome would come to me. I never forgot that first time.

"Is that Mister Darrell Brown?" the nurse asked.

"It is," I replied.

"I'm sorry, Mister Brown, but the result this time was unsuccessful. Hopefully we will have better luck next month." Click! That was the easy part. Then I had to tell my wife.

Weeks turned into months and months into years. I never completely got used to hearing the same message: "I'm sorry, Mister Brown, but once again you have been unsuccessful."

Often, I would be in the middle of a hectic shoot, and would have to leave set to take the call. Then I'd phone Jules and listen as she broke down in tears on the other end. After she calmed down, I'd walk back to my position behind the camera. No one around me had a clue about what had just happened. As difficult as it was for me, my heart went out to Jules. Many nights, she would cry herself to sleep. Those quiet moments of desperation became all-consuming. I felt helpless—not a great feeling for a husband who promised to be her provider.

We did our best to remain positive about creating a family.. We even discussed the possibility of moving into a bigger place. I had invited Jim, the local real estate agent, to give us an appraisal on the house. We were sitting in the kitchen sipping tea and talking about the current state of the market. When my phone rang, I instantly recognised the clinic's number. Jules was in the bedroom and, unknown to me, was listening intently. I had forgotten, but she knew exactly what day it was, and had a pretty good idea who was calling—in fact, was expecting it.

"Is this Mister Brown?" the nurse asked, as usual.

"Yes it is," I replied.

"Mister Brown, we are calling to let you know that your procedure this month was successful."

"I'm sorry?" I needed a double-take.

"Your wife is pregnant."

I slowly put the phone to my chest and smiled at Jim. I asked him if he was finished with the appraisal and, if so, he could let himself out. I told him this was an important personal call. Once Jim had left, I asked if the nurse could repeat what she had just said. She confirmed that, indeed, Jules was now pregnant. The "magical" day had arrived: my sperm and her eggs had finally met.

Knowing you have information that, once shared, will completely change someone's life is a surreal and wonderful moment. For me, that moment was like knowing I had just won the first-division Lotto and was about to break the news to the woman I loved. I hung up the phone and slowly made my way to the bedroom. I became acutely aware of the significance of the moment. The news I was about to break to Jules would change her life forever. All those sleepless nights, the crying and heartache, the worry and the pain of not knowing, were finally over. I had the words that would take away her pain—all I had to do was walk in and share it.

When I first entered the room, I couldn't see her. "Jules," I yelled. Then, peering over the bed I saw her, cowered up into a ball, hands over her face. She lifted her head and looked at me, waiting for the news. She knew who had been on the phone and had heard parts of the conversation. Finally, she had a glimmer of hope that the moment we had been praying for had arrived. But a part of her was still unsure. How would she cope if she had misheard the call? What if the result was negative yet again? How could she possibly go on?

"You're pregnant," I blurted out.

I'll never forget the cry that came from her—a primal scream of someone who had just had the weight of the world taken off her shoulders. The cry of a mother who had been given the ultimate blessing. She cried uncontrollably while I nestled next to her trying to give as much physical comfort as I could. Finally, when she gathered herself together, she looked at me and said, "I don't believe you. I need to hear it for myself!" She ran to the phone and called the clinic.

"Yes, Misses Brown, that's right. Congratulations, you're pregnant!"

*

I arrived at the hospital earlier than expected. I couldn't wait to see Jules and stroke that little bump I had been talking to for the past nine months. As I walked through the doors, I remember thinking, *the next time I see the outside world, I will be a dad.*

For many men, perhaps a daunting thought, but for some reason not me, I never for a moment doubted my ability to be a good father. Of course I knew there would be difficult times as well, but on the whole, I felt well prepared for the journey.

I'll never forget the moment he arrived. I stood at one end of the bed with Jules, the doctor and nurse at the other end behind a raised sheet. Like a magician pulling a rabbit out of a hat, the doctor raised one hand above the sheet and up sprung my little boy. Covered in fluids and crying his lungs out, he never looked more beautiful. After quickly being cleaned up, he arrived on Jules' breast and together we stared fixed in a semi-hypnotic trance…a sea of love and a dream finally come true.

As I looked into his eyes, I couldn't help thinking how hard this fella had tried to get here. Although he had only been in this world a few seconds, already he made both of us the happiest people on Earth.

Little Cody Joshua Squire Brown was born.

5

COMING HOME

The night before we brought Cody home from the hospital for the first time I could barely contain my excitement, and stayed up most of the night. Like most couples, Jules and I had spent a lot of time preparing the nursery and getting the house ready. The day before, I had decided to go to the local news agency to buy a dozen of the largest sheets of white paper I could find. I stuck them together with sticky tape to make one giant banner, and wrote in giant letters: "Welcome Home, Cody!" I stuck the banner up outside on the front of the house. Most of the neighbours already knew about our new arrival but nonetheless I still wanted to shout it to the world. I even blew up balloons and stuck them to the sign.

When we finally arrived home, I told Jules to wait while I got out my video camera. She had no idea about the sign, so when she finally emerged from the car with our firstborn son, you can imagine her surprise. I still have the footage.

I did the same thing for Taylor, our second son, who arrived just thirteen months later—a result of natural consequences!

From the books I was reading, I learned much about the impact of the environment on a newborn baby. Even in the earliest stages of pregnancy, the structure of the unborn child's brain can be greatly affected by their surroundings. This, of course, includes the emotional state of the mother. As a father of an unborn child, you can be fooled into thinking there's not much for you to do. Deep down we all know that's not true. I knew that Jules' emotional state played an important role in the biological unfolding of our little one. While Jules made sure to eat healthy, refrain from drinking alcohol, or allowing any other toxins into her body, I knew I could contribute by making sure her world was as peaceful and loving as possible. I didn't want her to get upset or get into any heated arguments. Naturally, I'm not suggesting we didn't have our disagreements, of course we did; some days did test our patience. But, in general, things were calm and caring in our household.

One of Jules' favourite times during each of her pregnancies was winter. I would light the log fire in our lounge room, and we would sit stroking her tummy while the warmth of the crackling flames heated the room. She didn't even seem to mind that Friday night football was on (which might also explain the two football-obsessed young boys we have today).

As a dad, I was hands-on right from the start. I changed the boys' nappies, and continued to do so until they were toilet trained. I loved rubbing and cuddling their little bodies. It became a morning ritual for me to get up early and go into their room and get them. I would change those smelly nappies, wash the boys down, and sprinkle baby powder on their bums while they giggled and smiled the whole time. Then I would bring them into Jules and we would lie in bed and cuddle and kiss them—bathing them in a sea of love.

All this time, their young brains were growing the way that nature intended. Without any fear of a dangerous or hostile environment, they were free to grow, thousands of brand-new nerve connections sprouted every minute. Their brain structures and immune systems were helping to create two healthy, young specimens of the human race.

But something just as important was also happening for Jules and me. As I discovered becoming a parent involves a highly important biological function. As much as a child reaches out to its parent for support during its growth process, the arrival of a baby plays a crucial role in the growth of the adults. We now know that nature also has a plan for adults: our own biological unfolding kicks into gear when we become parents.

After leaving home as young, fresh-faced teenagers (or most likely in our early twenties these days!), we go forth into the world forging out careers, bringing our fresh creative ideas to the workplace, trying to make a difference. We strive for success in business and search for an occupation that meets our desires. We travel to faraway countries, make new friends, and do our best to find our place in the world. If we are fortunate enough we find a partner, buy a home, and even create some kind of financial security. We gather wisdom and take much from our experiences, and, perhaps, search for some deeper meaning and out spiritual place in the larger scheme.

Parenting is part of nature's plan to help us through an important stage of our evolution into adulthood. Becoming a parent is the ultimate selfless act (or should be). The newborn child comes to us completely helpless and vulnerable. It requires our undivided attention. It *demands* our attention! It pulls out of us that deep desire to love unconditionally. Nothing else can ever bring about such a profound response to life. This is by no means an accident.

The arrival of a baby is at the same time the arrival of the servant parent—perhaps the greatest spiritual journey one can ever embark on. After all, one has only to look at enlightened spiritual leaders to see they were always guided by the mantra, "How may I serve?" Surely then, the gift of becoming a parent holds within it the highest of human rewards.

Of course, there are many for whom being a parent isn't part of their life's journey. For some, it's a conscious choice; for others, circumstances simply didn't allow it. However, even without children of your own, opportunities to invest your life into other people's children's are readily available—whether they are nieces and nephews, your neighbours' kids, or simply ones you meet at the park. All of us were once children, and we always responded well to a friendly face, a kind voice, or a friendly smile. It takes just one conversation to change a child's life. It might be a conversation with you.

6

WILD AT HEART

"The Margaret River house" is the name we gave to my brother's vacant property, three hours' drive south of Perth and just south of the beautiful tourist town of Margaret River itself. We first took Cody down there when Jules was six months pregnant. He was just a bump in her tummy, but for us he was the focus of almost every conversation.

We wanted to ground our boys in nature as early as possible; even though he wasn't yet born, we knew this environment would help with the pregnancy.

The Margaret River house was a two-story log cabin made of heavy stone and timber. Nestled among ten hectares of natural forest, it made an ideal hideaway for Jules and me to come and relax. In the years ahead, it also became the perfect place for us to grow closer to our boys.

I once attended a talk by a spiritual psychologist who spoke about how indigenous cultures throughout the ages have used ceremony to connect their children to the land. He said that if you don't ground your children in nature, when they get older, they won't know what to do with their suffering. He was absolutely right. His wisdom has remained with me down through the years.

At a 2013 Australian conference on Men's Health, keynote speaker Warren Farrell stated in his opening address, "There is a crisis in boys in Australia today." Unfortunately many of our teenage boys are confused, lonely, and anxious. Our boys are being medicated en masse for all sorts of mental illnesses, such as ADHD, Body Dysmorphia and Depression. Statistics out of the US state that suicide as of the year 2000 is now the third highest cause of all deaths in children between the ages of five and seventeen. – Staggering!

So many young kids today don't know what to do with their suffering. Sadly, many parents don't know either. Perhaps, as a result of modelling their parents, large numbers of teenagers suffer in silence as they try alcohol, drugs, and medication to numb the pain of being disconnected from the world around them.

In *The Biology of Transcendence*, Joseph Chilton Pearce suggests that the current epidemic in teenage suicide in the Western world is a modern-day phenomenon. Never before in recorded history have so many of our young boys wanted to leave this planet at such a young age. It's a sign that we're in a lot of trouble. And it has been growing for decades. As a result of my own research, I was acutely aware of the problems facing children even before our boys were born. Jules and I were determined not to repeat the pattern with our kids.

The Margaret River house became our constant escape from the chaos that comes from spending too much time in the city.

Its remoteness gave us the peace and we loved being surrounded by the beauty of nature. From the moment we pulled off the gravel road onto the mile-long driveway, we could already smell the crisp, fresh scent emanating from the tall jarrah trees that lined the bumpy track leading down the winding road to the house.

So many things about this place made it special.

Over the years, many of our friends used to come down and spend weekends with us at the house. The isolation, peace, and quiet would often change people. Fortunately, the place is remote enough that no television, internet, or mobile phone coverage is available. This made our hideaway a challenging environment for some people—but not for us. Many people like to think they are not addicted to technology. But try turning it off. In this house, visitors had no other option but to go without their gadgets. As a result, it meant that each evening the *people* became the focus for each other. Silence and isolation can really test people. Without the distractions of modern technology, many people often don't know what to do with their time. Instead of losing themselves in Facebook, email, browsing websites or watching movies, they have to learn to *be with* other people. Most of all, though, they have to learn to be with themselves.

The distinct lack of distractions was great for the boys, however. It forced them to use their imaginations and to find their own fun. For the boys, this was no trouble at all. The creek running through the back of the property became their wonderland. Their favourite pastime was catching the tadpoles living in the large ponds that formed in winter time. On any given day, we could catch up to a hundred tadpoles, only to release them again at the end of the day. Making sure to return whatever they caught back to its natural environment was one of the lessons we taught our boys.

The rustic house was completely surrounded by windows that allowed the sun to stream into most rooms when it broke through the trees in the morning. Each day would begin with a stroll through the property along the well-worn paths that meandered through the lush surrounding forest.

As our boys grew into toddlers, these routine walks through the forest introduced them to their connection with nature. I used to ask the boys questions about the world around them and would explain that the trees grow straight upwards toward the sun because they need the energy of sunlight to grow and become strong. Being in nature does the same for humans, too, I would tell them. We need fresh air, the elements and the light, and the beauty of the outdoors to help us grow in strength.

If a leaf floated down past their faces, I would explain that it would soon dissolve into the ground and eventually provide nutrients for other plants to live on. I pointed out that one day they, too, would be given back to the earth; this allowed them to see that they were also part of the greater cycle of life.

They loved hearing how things worked in the great exchange of life. I would tell them how the trees give off oxygen so we can breathe. We need them as much as they need us. Trees "inhale" the carbon-dioxide we exhale, to complete the cycle. We need to learn to respect the natural world, as well as each other, in order to live together in a healthy environment. Without green plants, we wouldn't survive.

Over the last 20 years, the landscape of childhood had changed dramatically. It's hard to believe, but the latest research tells us that children now spend close to an incredible 90 percent of their time indoors. A little anecdote illustrates this: A mother encouraged her little boy to go play outside and he protested: "But there aren't any power outlets in the garden!" To him, play meant plugging in some electronic gadget. This transformation is happening now right before our eyes and, unfortunately, many parents feel completely helpless in the face of this onslaught from the digital world.

The average child today spends between five and fifteen hours a day staring at screens. More and more children are interacting with a virtual environment at the expense of the real one outside. At some point in time, we parents must start to ask: What are the consequences of a childhood removed from nature?

Sometimes, friends would come down to the house with their kids and we would all head off on a walk through the forest. The grownups would rigorously insist that their kids put on their boots before walking out the front door. Seeing our boys run out of the house with bare feet surprised them. Our friends would look at me and ask if my boys needed shoes, and proceed to explain how dangerous the bush was. "What if they get splinters from the sticks, or step on a snake?"

I agreed that these things were always possible, although in fifteen years I had never seen a single snake at the property. We were so far south that the cold weather wasn't a suitable environment for snakes. Let's not forget that for thousands of years, indigenous people seem to manage just fine walking on the wild land without shoes. It was important for the boys to feel the ground under their feet, to squish the mud between their toes and let the soles of their feet harden to the land. On some occasions the boys would wear their boots, but when we went to the creek to catch the tadpoles, any footwear had to come off.

On one particular occasion, I took some family friends down to the creek so the kids could catch tadpoles. When we arrived, my boys waded knee-high straight into the cold creek water, which would eventually numb any feeling in their toes. They would immediately start to fill their glass jars with as many little critters as they could find. However, the mother of the other family would not allow her children to remove their shoes at all. Instead, they had to sit and watch from the side while our boys had all the fun.

"I'm sorry kids, but you have no idea what's in the bottom of that creek!" she explained. *That's exactly right*, I thought, she didn't know. Unfortunately, now, neither do the kids. For some strange reason, the mud at the bottom of our creek was risky, but violent video games and internet chat rooms are fine? How upside-down our habits and preferences have become!

Walking along the tracks, I would encourage the boys to use their peripheral vision. I asked them to look up, across, and down. I wanted them to see the different worlds happening all around us. Above, high up in the trees, lived the birds, the possums, and a lot of other tree life. At eye level, we could see kangaroos, native shrubs, and wild flowers. Down at our feet, the ground was dotted with insects, puddles, fallen leaves, and fungi. Each world appeared separate from the other, and yet all of them remain intricately connected.

As a photographer, I would always bring my camera with me on these walks. I used macro lenses to photograph the unique environments that lived below the tree stumps. The early morning sun provided excellent back lighting for my shots of the wonderfully colourful fungi and insects. I would spend the evenings bringing the photos to life on my laptop. Engrossed in a slideshow of colour, I would go through the photos with the boys, pointing out the patterns in nature that replicated themselves through every environment. The spirals on the shells washed up on the beach seemed to exactly match the spirals on the snails under the logs. The cobwebs left behind by the spiders looked just like the patterns in the stars of the Milky Way.

Most boys learn about nature in the classroom. If most boys were students like me, the classroom education didn't mean much. There's no real reference point for the information to connect to. Walking through the forest, in stark contrast, allowed the boys to experience nature firsthand and find their place in it. It had meaning, it had feeling, and now it had purpose.

As the boys got older, our walks through the forest became more of an adventure. We would pretend we were the "Lords of the Rings." Each of us had our own magical staff that we had painted and glued on sparkling letters that spelled our names. Boys love to believe in magic and mysticism, and Jules and I always encouraged imagination. The Margaret River house was a great place for a magical adventure.

In *Wild at Heart*, author John Eldredge suggests that in the heart of every boy lies a warrior. The father's role is to help bring that out and shape it for good. I aimed to show our boys how to fight for justice and to battle the bad guys. I guess I tried to show them with my own life that to serve others is right and noble.

In recent years we have begun emasculating our young boys by telling them not to play with guns, bows and arrows, or to play make-believe war games. But such restrictions run against their evolutionary instincts. Males are biologically wired to fight to protect our loved ones. In young boys, this shows up as a natural inclination for adventure. From an evolutionary perspective, boys are wired for aggression and displays of strength—and the best place for that to come out is in play.

However, modern "civilized" society tries to suppress this natural instinct in young males (except in times of war or perhaps the football field). Influenced by society, I made this mistake myself when my boys were younger. I remember my father kindly offering to take my boys to the royal show one year. As he rarely had time with the boys, Jules and I were happy for any chance for them to spend time with their granddad. When they returned home later that evening, the boys proudly showed off the show bags that Granddad had brought for them. I noticed that one of the bags contained a set of guns, which the boys had played with. I explained to Dad that we don't let the boys play with guns, and suggested he keep them for another time. Looking back, I now regret that decision.

One weekend down at the Margaret River house, as the boys were entering their teenage years, I asked them if they wanted to make their own bows and arrows—capable of shooting a wooden arrow thirty meters into the side of a tree with great precision. The look of excitement on the boys' faces meant I didn't have to ask twice. First, we needed to make the bows. I took Cody and Taylor to a part of the property where some young trees had sprouted out of the creek bed. I knew these saplings had great flexibility and would be easily bent into the shape of a bow.

Getting the string for the bow meant a journey into town to the local hardware store, where we also purchased a couple of meters of doweling to make the arrows. However, the final stop intrigued the boys most. As I pulled up in front of the sports shop, the boys were very keen to know why we were there. I walked in and asked the guy if he had any dart flights. Fortunately, he did. I explained to the boys that the dart flights would be fixed to the back of the arrows to help them fly straight and true after they left the bow. Their faces beamed with excitement; this was going to be a serious bow and arrow set.

Once back at the house, the boys helped to bend the young sticks into bows while I pulled the string taut around both ends. I gave the boys a knife and asked them to sharpen the ends of each arrow to a fine point while I cut a groove in the opposite end and wedged in the dart flights. Once finished, I showed them how to fire the arrows. They practiced firing at a target I had placed high up on a tree until they became comfortable with their weapons of choice. Both Cody and Taylor were amazed at how deep the arrows were able to penetrate the bark, and smiled proudly as they had to use both hands to pull out each arrow.

I made sure to talk to them about the responsibility that comes with holding such a powerful implement. They should never point the arrows at each other, and to make sure no one was ever ahead of them when they aimed or fired. As we walked into the forest to slay the dragons, Taylor asked, "Hey Dad, what if we see a kangaroo? Can we fire at it?

"Well Taylor, think of it this way. Imagine you saw a kangaroo and fired at it and shot it through the stomach. Then, as you got closer to the kangaroo, you suddenly realised not only you had shot the arrow through the 'roos stomach, but also punctured its pouch as well, impaling a baby joey inside, piercing its head. As a direct result of your shot, both mother and baby are both left bleeding profusely, lying on the ground, terrified and in agony?"

I wanted to paint a dramatic picture to capture his imagination.

"Oh...I see what you mean."

I knew Taylor had a loving heart and a deep connection to animals. I could have just told him not to shoot at kangaroos, but instead I wanted to connect his mind to the possible consequences of his actions. I guess at first the idea sounded like fun; he simply hadn't thought it through.

Our log house was also home to a family of possums who performed a nightly ritual of climbing down the roof, along the windowsill, and onto their special mound of rocks where we left them food scraps. Whenever we brought friends down to stay at the house, the possums would always be one of the highlights of their stay. We would throw off-cuts of fruit and vegetables on top of the rock pile at the base of large jarrah tree, just meters from the back door.

My brother was a biologist, so he knew that by fixing a red light onto the roof outside and focusing it at the pile of rocks, it would allow people to watch the possums feed at night without scaring them away.

Late one afternoon in spring, while walking up to the side entrance of the house, I reached forward to open the back door and almost put my left hand on a baby possum clinging to the side of the cobbled wall. It scared the hell out of me. Apparently, it had strayed from its nest, as ordinarily it wouldn't be out during daytime.

After wrapping him in a soft towel, the boys took great delight in holding the little fella while we thought about the best way of returning him to his family. This kind of raw contact with nature leads boys to a deep connection with all living things. There's something spiritual about being close to wild animals not shut up in a cage. Later that evening, just before the family of possums came down, we took the little fella out to the rock pile and let him go. To our delight, he was quickly reconnected with his brood, and soon returned to his rightful place on his mum's back.

At night, we would sit in front of the open log fire and listen to old Dean Martin records. Monopoly, Scrabble, and UNO were all part of the evening's entertainment. We would ask the boys what they thought the best part of each day was, and then talk about the special things we would do tomorrow. It's good for children to have something to look forward to.

No one ever wanted our Margaret River holidays to end. Why wasn't our whole life like our holidays? Why do we spend forty-eight weeks a year looking forward to the other four? Somehow, it doesn't make sense. If I could share just one piece of wisdom with my boys from all this it was, it would be: *Great success comes from doing what you love.* People who love what they do never need a holiday. They just take them anyway.

Every time I packed the car for the drive home, my thoughts returned to the digital world we were taking our boys back to. Knowing what lay ahead in the city, I was glad they had a healthy appreciation for nature.

The words of Charles Jordon come to mind: "What children will not value, they will not protect, and what they will not protect, they will eventually lose."

Driving away from the house at the end of each holiday always filled us with mixed emotions. No one said very much on the return trip. In silence, we would individually reminisce about the wonderful time we had spent together. The boys would open the car windows to catch one last sniff of the fresh air, their eyes searching for a last chance spot of a kangaroo or lizard sitting on the side of the road, perhaps waiting to say goodbye.

As the tadpoles were growing into frogs, so too were our boys growing into young men.

7

BEING THERE

The clock on the wall was just about to tick over to 3.00 PM. Most guys I knew didn't finish work until at least five; some didn't get home until after seven. I remember recently sitting in a boardroom listening to two men talk about the long hours they had been working. One was sharp and young, a partner in an advertising agency I was doing some work for. The other was his client, the CEO of a company that manufactures kitchen stoves and associated appliances.

The CEO mentioned he had been starting work before 6.00 AM and not getting home until after 8.00 PM at night. However, not to be outdone, my agency friend explained that not only had he been working similar hours, but he was also bringing work home with him that he continued after dinner. You could see they both wore their long hours as some sort of badge of honour.

My silence in these conversations probably said more than any words could. Instead, my thoughts drifted off in the direction of my two boys and what they might be doing right now without me. I looked across at the CEO and saw a picture of his family sitting next to the computer on his desk. His wife had gifted him with five beautiful children. Knowing how much time I spent with my two boys, I knew that five must have been a big responsibility. I wondered if he knew his children as well as he knew his business.

My agency friend was also married and had two young children of his own. He had arrived that morning in his new two-door silver sports car. I had asked him somewhat jokingly how he managed to squeeze his two kids into the back seat. He had replied with a smile, "Only just!" I remember thinking about how difficult it would be for their little faces to peer out of those tiny windows—the world rushing by and no way to see it.

Sadly, today many men are becoming more detached from their children at a time when they are needed more than ever. So many men now put corporate success before their family. Somewhere, our culture took a turn down the wrong path, and I think we're way past that point when we should all realise we are now going the wrong way.

The clock moved towards 3.15 PM, signalling my favourite time of day. I loved being home when the boys arrived from school. It's an experience only shared by a small group of extremely fortunate fathers. I could always hear their footsteps as they came running down the driveway and along the side of the house. If I timed it right, I could walk out of my office just as they ran straight into my arms.

"Daddy! Daddy!" they would scream. Their small, lightly-framed bodies would catapult forward and collide into mine with a thud. Of course, it wasn't the force of their little bodies that hit me; it was the power of love deep inside. If I wasn't careful, it could knock me off my feet. Who would have thought love could be so strong?

It's funny how nature can sometimes become a metaphor for your own life. Sitting outside on the back porch one night, I found myself staring at a couple of moths dancing around a light globe. The moths appeared totally mesmerised by the light, the warmth, the brightness, and the glow. They would leave the light momentarily to venture off into the darkness only to return quickly and slam right back into the shining globe.

That was me. I was the light … and my boys were the moths.

On many occasions, Jules and I would just sit together staring at the boys while they played innocently in the playground. Sometimes she would reach across and wipe away a tear from my cheek. She knew how much I loved them. It was nice not to have to use words. That's what makes our relationship so special. We know each other so well.

If there's anything more powerful in this world than the love you feel for your children, I haven't discovered it yet. As with all experiences, you can't feel anyone else's love, just your own. Someone can tell you how much they love you, but all you can ever feel is the love you have in return. Since the boys gave me the opportunity to feel the deepest love imaginable, it felt natural to want to spend most of my waking hours around them.

To love this deeply is to find your life's purpose. Anything beyond that is a bonus, and can only ever take second place. Even finding a cure for cancer wouldn't measure up. Perhaps if we all could experience a love this pure, there wouldn't be any cancer.

As a freelance cameraman, I would usually average about three to four days of work a week. I liked it because I could make a good wage and still have plenty of time to spend with the family. Some people used to ask me why I didn't start my own production company or expand my talents into other areas. The truth is, I could never think of anything to do with my time that would be more valuable than being with my boys. Sure, the extra money would have been nice. But at the end of the day, it seemed so insignificant compared to the responsibility I had taken on as a father. Many years stretched ahead of me, years in which I could make money. But time with our children is lost with every passing day.

Besides, I had never heard of any father lying on his deathbed saying, "If only I'd had made more money." More often than not, their biggest regret was that they didn't spend more time with their children. This was something I would never have to worry about. My boys became my life. They were like oxygen. I needed them to breathe.

8

THE TREEHOUSE

The view from our kitchen window allows us to see straight out over the back fence and into a wonderfully inspiring, sloping bushland, filled with nature's gifts of lush native plants, singing bird life and spectacular wildflowers.

The back gate opens out onto twenty metres of sloping lawn kindly taken care of by the local council. This wonderful patch of green lawn, which doubles as the boy's football oval in winter and cricket pitch in summer, is really a mandatory firebreak from the "A class" bush reserve that our house in the beautiful suburb of Trigg backs onto.

Young boys should have the opportunity to connect with nature as often as possible. In today's technology-driven world that is unwittingly and yet slowly destroying the childhood of many young boys, living in a house that backs onto a reserve is a dream come true.

A very modest, three-bedroom brick home with a big shed out the back is more than enough to help make our family complete.

I awoke one cool winter's morning to see the frost still glistening on the leaves of the eucalyptus trees, backlit by the sun that bounces off the branches and streams in through our windows to greet us each day. I was inspired with an idea and rushed to my boys' room. "How would you like to look for a suitable tree to build a treehouse in?"

It's hard to describe the look of excitement on their wide-eyed faces as the suggestion of building a special treehouse with Dad began to sink in. It fell somewhere between the look you get on Christmas morning or a day at the Fair!

When I was a young boy, my brother and I used to play in the tree next to our rented house in the suburbs. Although we never actually built a treehouse, the tree itself played an important and enjoyable part in my life.

Scaling the tree's branches, I was suddenly able to expand my world. I could see far off into the backyards of the neighbouring houses and beyond. From that perspective, I didn't feel so isolated. That's what treehouses do. They give us another view on the world. For a young boy, it can often provide a moment of clarity. It shows him his kingdom in relation to other lands. Lands yet to be conquered and adventures yet to be had.

I often remember sitting up in the tree by myself just watching the world around me. It was a great place to be by myself—to sit, and think, and be.

In springtime, the tree bore a small cherry-like fruit that was poisonous to eat but made for great ammunition for the slingshot my brother and I made between two branches. Our target would often be the window of the house next door, and the splatter of red dye on the white wall would let us know whether to aim more to the left or to the right. Trees and boys will always equal fun and adventure.

The boys and I decided to build our treehouse in a bushy green willow tree about 20 meters to the left of our back gate. The willow stood in the middle of the firebreak, so it had a lot of regular traffic walking by underneath in the early morning and late afternoons. People would often walk their dogs on the grass, taking them right underneath the tree.

Cody, Taylor, and I would take great delight in sitting high up in the branches remaining completely quiet while the people walked by below, totally unaware of our presence above. It was the perfect spot for a treehouse.

From up there, we could see right into our neighbour's backyard. They would feed the white cockatoos each evening as they landed on their back fence. We found it easy to remain hidden while this daily ritual took place. The cockatoos knew we were there, but they didn't mind. They didn't feel threatened by our presence, nor should they have. From the time the boys first started walking, Julie and I used to take them on regular trips to the forest. That's where they learned to respect all that nature has to offer. The cockatoos knew this.

One of my spiritual teachers once asked me, "Are you comfortable in the silence?" Down at my brother's Margaret River house, I discovered what he meant. Silence is good for people. It's good for body, mind, and soul. It's especially good for young boys. In this sacred environment, the boys became grounded in nature, spiritually connected to the land, and eternally bonded with their dad. Without the distractions of the chaotic modern world, a boy can find himself more easily. In the silence, *there he is*.

Before building the treehouse, I got the boys to climb up with me and sit in the branches. Just sitting up there suddenly brought back so many fond memories of my own childhood. I asked them how they thought the treehouse should look and where we should start building.

Boys love to participate in building projects. It gives them ownership of the end product and also empowers them to be part of the design process. Any opportunity you get to stimulate their imaginations, take it.

As dads, we sometimes make the mistake of trying to do it all ourselves, usually because we think we will do a better and faster job. But boys don't care so much about that. They really want to spend time with their Dad, to show him what they can do. The greatest word a boy can hear from his dad is *"Let's . . ."* It's an invitation *to do something together*, and any time you do something with your boys, the bond between you grows stronger.

I asked them what sort of wood they thought we should use, where they thought the entrance should be, and if we should use a rope to help climb up. Did they want a slingshot? With their imaginations excited, the ideas just kept coming. I wanted to see how many ideas they could come up with and once we got to work, I tried hard to implement as many as I could. I wanted them both to feel they had as much input into the treehouse as I did.

We found some old pieces of timber in the shed to make a start, but soon realised we would need a whole lot more. Finding a treasure trove of old timber in a neighbour's shed was an unexpected bonus—another reason why it's good to be kind to your neighbours. We began to build. Slowly, the boys passed up the pieces of timber to me, one at a time. Some were measured and marked for sawing; others were nailed straight in. We also tried to include strong branches that had fallen in the forest so we could use as much from the natural environment as possible. We used thin wire to secure these pieces in place.

We ended up with a secure, three-level treehouse. We tied ropes above to give us something to hold onto while moving between the branches. It became a boy's true adventure playground. We even managed a slingshot and a telescope, and installed a rope ladder the boys could pull up at night.

There's something special about sitting in a treehouse with your boys. It allows you to enter their world, to break down the barriers of age. The challenge for us fathers is to remember what it was like to be a boy, and to be able to relive it again.

Letting go of your father-figure role and becoming a kid again can often be a challenge. Authoritarian fathers rarely show their emotions and aim to always be in control. To such men, the idea of climbing up into a treehouse with their kids would have been absurd. Treehouses are for children.

I think this attitude stems from the fact that many men today have been raised by fathers who forgot how to play. A lot of them may have lived through a war-time era, and lost their own childhood early on. They were constantly pressured to "grow up." So they did. Every day a father forgets how to be a kid, the world becomes a sadder place.

Treehouses help us break down barriers and allow us to be kids again. Boys love it when they see Dad as another member of their gang. It's especially good to let one of them be the leader, and for Dad to take the orders. I felt this type of role reversal empowered the boys and gave them a sense of responsibility.

Playtime allows this. Not until we leave the "real world" behind can the magic and imaginal world of "let's pretend" flourish.

On one occasion, sitting in the treehouse with Cody and Taylor, we noticed a young teenage lad off in the distance. He was walking toward us. Carrying a weighty school bag on his back, his face constantly looked down, as he dragged his feet along the ground. As he got closer I realised what was distracting him. He was absorbed in a computer game on his mobile phone, and the natural sounds of the world around him were blocked out by ear plugs attached to his iPod. The treehouse gave me opportunities to point out things about the world I wanted the boys to see.

As we silently watched the teenager walk beneath us, I seized the moment to offer some more wisdom to my two young warriors.

"Ok ... did anyone just see that?" I asked.

"You mean that boy who just walked past?" asked Taylor.

"Yes," I said. "Something very important just happened, and I don't want either of you to miss it."

"I know!" said Cody. "We have to be very careful not to drop anything that might hurt someone who walks underneath us."

That was true and a good response, but it wasn't the point I was hoping to make. I wanted them to notice something far more important than that. I asked the boys to keep very silent and listen to what they could hear. When you ask your children to be still and silent and to place their attention in a certain way, they suddenly become very present.

Most children do, in fact, spend a lot of time in the present moment. It's what they call "play." Children need to play—*a lot!*—certainly more than they need to do chores or homework. Play gives children control over their external world. It also allows for the higher cortical regions of their brain to develop, something that computer games and television have been scientifically shown to destroy.

"What can you hear?" I asked the boys. As if on cue, a symphony of bird noises began to play all around us. Up in a treehouse, you are with the birds. You share their space, and in doing so, expose yourself to the wonders of nature.

"Now what can you see?" I asked. We could see for miles from up there, and they reported seeing a great many things they might otherwise have missed from ground level.

I then pointed down at the young boy now walking off into the distance, still dragging his feet, shoulders hunched, and head down.

"See that boy?" I asked. "He's missing life. He can't see the beautiful flowers that he's treading on. He can't hear the sounds of the forest trying so hard to get his attention. And, worst of all, he walked right past this amazing treehouse and the chance to make some new friends." I could see my boys felt sad for that young fellow. How lucky they were, up in the treehouse with their dad. "Don't miss life, boys, whatever you do. Don't miss life."

We sat and watched the sun slowly setting over the forest. No more words were required.

And they thought we were just building a treehouse.

9

DO YOU BELIEVE?

"No I wasn't! Yes you were! No I'm not." The boys used to love playing cricket in the backyard. One day I walked outside to find them arguing over someone "being out." I thought they might need an umpire. That's when I heard those words that will stay with me forever:

"Anyway, Cody, you're not in charge," said Tay.

"Oh yeah," Cody replied, "then who is?"

Taylor paused and gathered his thoughts and said, "Mum, Dad, God, and Santa!"

Perhaps like a lot of people, December was always my favourite month of the year. As a young boy, it signalled many things. The end of school, the beginning of holidays, the start of summer, surfing at the beach, and, of course…Christmas.

I particularly loved the idea of Santa Claus and his flying reindeers skipping from rooftop to rooftop delivering presents to all the girls and boys. Growing up in a rented house with one parent meant that money was often scarce, so knowing that Santa was going to look after us with at least one present always left me with a wonderful feeling of excitement. Every child needs something to look forward to. It's what gets them through the difficult times.

Though we never seemed to have much money, somehow Santa always managed to drop some presents of at our place. He didn't discriminate, and never let us down. I remember waking up the Christmas morning that I was eight years old and running to see what Santa had left us under the tree. There it was in all its glory: a sparkling, shiny blue push bike, my first ever. It didn't matter that it was second-hand. A new coat of paint had made it sparkle, and all that mattered to me was *it was mine!*

If climbing trees in my backyard allowed me to see into other kingdoms, then a bike gave me the freedom to go explore them. And explore we did.

My brother and sister were fortunate to also receive bikes that Christmas morning, so the three of us immediately decided to go on an adventure and criss-cross the neighbourhood. I remember an overwhelming sense of freedom as I took off down the street. I could feel the wind on my face as my feet began to pedal as fast as they could. The houses rushed by faster than ever before; I could outpace dogs, and jump over curbs. I got up so much speed that I could lift my feet and watch as the pedals went round and round by themselves. We rode down streets we had never been down before, simply because they were there. Suddenly, things didn't seem so far away anymore. We rode to a nearby lake and when we got there, we decided to ride all the way around it. Nothing could stop us; we were out of range of Dad's voice. Now we were making our own decisions. I was eight going on eighteen; the smile on my face had never been bigger and my life had never been brighter.

When we finally returned home, it was way past lunch. The turkey had gone cold, and poor Dad was waiting there by himself. We had been away for hours and had totally lost track of time. It all seemed very surreal, as I sat at the table my heart was still pounding, and although I was hungry I couldn't wait to get back on my bike. That night, I slept with my bike next to my bed. Could this be real? How could I be so lucky? I never imagined Christmas could so wonderful.

As much as I enjoyed Christmas as a boy, becoming a father gave the holiday a whole new meaning. Every year, on the first day of December, we would take the boys to cut down our own Christmas tree, a tradition we have continued for twenty years. Everyone told us it was cheaper to buy a plastic one and simply reuse it each year. But that wasn't us. Plastic wasn't real, and Christmas had to be real. There's nothing plastic about the smell of pine that permeates the house at Christmas time. We always tried to find the biggest and proudest looking tree. And, along with their mum, the boys loved decorating the branches, as she passed out the tinsel, baubles, and fairy lights.

Christmas was a time of magic and make believe, of Santa Claus and flying reindeers. It was a time of fairy tales and chocolate Santas, of eggnog and Christmas carols. The boys used to love walking the neighbourhood looking at the festive lights that adorned the nearby houses. They would look up to the sky and try to spot Santa's sleigh. On Christmas Eve, we would leave milk and cookies out for Santa at the bottom of the fireplace. We would even leave carrot sticks and water outside for the reindeer.

One time, I suggested to the boys that we leave a piece of blank white paper next to the carrots to see if the reindeer left any footprints. When the boys fell asleep, I cut a potato into the shape of reindeer hooves, then dipped them in crushed coffee and a few drops of water, and patted hoof marks onto the paper. In the morning, after spotting the half-eaten cookies and empty glass of milk, the boys hurried outside and, to their amazement, saw the evidence of Santa's reindeers. That was all the proof they needed. For them, all of it was real—just as it should be.

One day, the boys came to Jules and me to say that a friend's mom had said that Santa wasn't real. We always knew it was just a matter of time before these questions would arise. Our answer was short and simple: "Well boys, you see Santa is only real if you believe in him. Your mum and I believe in Santa just as much as we believe in Christmas. Of course, he is real." With that, the boys smiled and life could return to normal.

Many parents have convinced themselves that somehow kids need to be told some sort of "truth" about Santa. They worry they will be caught in some sort of lie. When did life become so black and white? When did they leave behind the world of magic and fantasy? After all, "Santa" is of course, just a word… it's everything that he represents that's real.

The key to life is to live in the mystery, to inhabit and explore the grey areas, to believe in the magic of life where anything is possible. What does it actually mean to believe in Santa Claus? It means you believe that childhood is magical; that fairies ride on the wings of little girls and that boys can fight pirates in their backyard tree house. It means that dreams can come true, and that sometimes the things that matter to us most are the things we can't see. Santa Claus is symbolic of the pure joy and innocence of childhood. Why on Earth would I ever stop believing in him?

In today's society, we expect adults to behave in certain ways. For example, we are supposed to be "responsible," "logical," and measured in our approach to life. The workplace demands such qualities, and rewards those who comply. The world of work is black and white, and separates the grownups from their children. Our beliefs become more rigid, and we focus on being "sensible." We learn to value things that are tangible, which can be calculated on a spreadsheet—these things, we are told, are what's "real," what matters. But that's a joyless approach to life.

As we become more socially conditioned in our grownup years, we wonder why life seems to lose its joy, its mystery and excitement. We look back to our childhood as the happier times, when anything was possible and simple things filled us with wonder. In childhood, imagination was king. It was a time when we dreamed of things beyond this world. The boundaries between what was real and what was possible were blurred, and all options were still on the table.

Does it have to be this way? Do we have to lose the magic? I'm not convinced. The science of quantum physics shows that everything in the universe is connected. The deeper scientists began to explore the quantum world inside atoms, and they continued to find smaller and smaller "particles." When they hit "bottom" and detected individual quanta, they saw that our solid world of matter is, ultimately, made up of vibrating packets of energy. That's what a quantum is—*a vibrating bundle of energy*—and it's what our world is made of. Even more intriguing is the awareness that everything is interconnected to everything else. In the end, then, we are all nothing but vibrations of energy.

At the other extreme, in the large-scale world of stars and galaxies, science shows that the universe is expanding and might continue to do so forever. Whether we look at the world through a microscope or a telescope, nature gives us the same message: At the micro- and macro-levels, our world is full of mysteries, revealing a universe that seems as endless "all the way down" as it is infinite "all the way up." Either way, the more we look, the more we discover that the universe outside is as endless as the universe inside…and we are all connected.

The more science pushes forward, the more we realise that things we can't find on a spreadsheet are just as real as the things we can. In other words, reality consists of non-measurable things—minds, intentions, and choices—as well as measurable objects such as brains, buckets, and blocks of marble. As Einstein famously put it, "Not everything that counts can be counted; and not everything that can be counted, counts." Some of the most important aspects of life cannot be captured in figures—such as love, imagination, volition, choice, emotions, or feelings of any kind.

I think the most courageous way to grow up is to hold onto the beliefs that served us well when we were young. Don't ever forget what it was like to be a child because you will lose the greatest way you have to connect with your children. The things that you believed back then that made your world so wonderful will be the same for your children today. Stop telling them to "grow up" and start encouraging them to "grow out"—to expand their world through dreams and imagination, to be creative and wild in their aspirations, to believe that anything is possible and everything is achievable.

No one ever said it so beautifully as the British Romantic poet Samuel Taylor Coleridge:

What if you slept...and what if in your sleep you dreamed, and what if in your dream you went to heaven. And there you plucked a strange and beautiful flower, and what if when you woke you held that flower in your hand ...ah...what then?

10

A WORLD GONE MAD

Months had passed since we built the treehouse, and over time its legendary status had grown. Kids would ride their bikes from far afield to get a glimpse of this playground treasure. Every now and then, we would watch as kids passed by the treehouse with their parents. The children would scramble to climb up the rope while the parents would call them back, "No, no. It's not yours. Don't go up there." We would quickly rush out and explain that it was fine and that their children were more than welcome to climb the treehouse.

After a time, we decided to build a sign and nailed it to the base of the tree. It read:

> Welcome to Cody and Taylor's Secret Treehouse.
> Feel Free to Climb Up and Have Fun.
> Please Take Care at All Times!

Language is very important; everything about the sign had to be welcoming, but at the same time, we wanted people to be responsible.

The parents would often comment on how wonderful the treehouse was and how much their kids looked forward to coming over to play. One woman told us that she thought the treehouse was a godsend. "I could never get my son to come and walk the dog with me, until I told him about your treehouse. Now he comes with me nearly every day. It's the only thing that gets him off his computer!"

I recall some families bringing picnic blankets and sandwiches. As word grew of the treehouse, it became a local attraction. "We've come to see the famous treehouse," people would say. I decided to improve on the attraction. I found an old tyre and bought a long yellow rope. I made a swing that hung from one of the bigger branches, strong enough to take the weight of three kids at a time.

I remember one dad pushing his three daughters all at once. The laughter of those little girls could be heard clearly from our kitchen window. What more could a family ask for? While their mum sat on the blanket, cutting a cake into pieces, her husband was pushing his three little girls effortlessly on the swing. They giggled and tried to hang on—each push taking them higher off the ground. They leaned so far back their long golden hair nearly touched the ground. All this fun, and it didn't cost him a cent.

The tree was adorned with toy dinosaurs and dragons nailed to various branches. We added ropes and planks to allow the children to climb higher. The boys loved the challenge, whereas the girls often found comfort at the first level. Jules decided it would be good to add some fairies for the girls to enjoy, while the slingshot was always a hit with the young lads.

Some days we would arrive to find a few of the toys broken or damaged. Dinosaurs had been ripped out and thrown to the ground; sometimes they were gone completely. At first, our boys used to get upset and found it hard to understand why kids would come and vandalise such a wonderful treehouse. I explained that unfortunately life was like that. Perhaps whoever did it was just angry at life. Perhaps things weren't too happy for them at home and they had taken out their frustration on the treehouse. For them, maybe the treehouse served another purpose: a place where kids could vent their frustrations about things that weren't working well in their lives. Nonetheless, everyone was still welcome. We never let the damaged toys stop us from rebuilding our fortress of fun.

More important for my boys, they learned to shrug it off, and we would race back to the shed to the big crate that stored our supply of dinosaurs. As little boys, Cody and Taylor used to love lining up their dinosaurs on the carpet floor ready for battle. It didn't take too many birthdays and Christmases to build up a big supply. We would grab a handful from the crate and race back to the tree. With a pocket full of nails and a hammer in tow, we scaled the branches and went about nailing a new "herd" of dinosaurs to the branches. The treehouse was a wonderland that allowed our kids' imagination to take over. One day they were pirates; the next they were soldiers. It allowed for those life-affirming experiences that all children require.

Being high up in the tree also came with a sense of uncertainty. Although the planks and ropes were secure, the kids still had to think about how they navigated the branches. Always holding on with one hand, either to a rope or a branch, climbing became an exciting mixture of fun and physical challenge: keeping safe, yet enjoying the uncertainty. Most playgrounds today forego the uncertainty. The homogenized attractions built by the local council are all about safety. Perhaps they're fun at first, but kids quickly lose interest. After a while, all the playgrounds look the same. I think that's what attracted so many to our treehouse. It was different. It was an adventure. It constantly changed, and it was never built to be "safe."

However, little did I know then, it was all about to change.

One frosty winter's morning after dropping the boys at school, I heard a knock at the door. Through the window, I could see a gentleman wearing a green uniform and holding a clipboard in his right hand. I curiously opened the door to see a slightly built man standing with his back to me.

"Hi there, can I help you?" I asked.

"Yes, you can," he replied, turning around to face me. "I was wondering if you could tell me who that treehouse out the back of your place belongs to?"

Immediately, I felt a sinking feeling in my stomach.

The A-class reserve our house backed onto was the same bush reserve that Jules had grown up next to as a little girl. Her mum and dad still lived on the same street as us and she often told me about her childhood years with her brother and sister, running off into the bush and building cubbies and treehouses. Gone for most of the day, they would return only to be fed and watered and then run back to continue their adventures—as we all did as children. It was part of growing up in the suburbs of Western Australia. But not anymore.

"Well," I said, "I guess the truth is that treehouse belongs to everyone," I replied to the man, who, according to the embroidery on his shirt, was from the local council.

"But if you're asking who built it? Well, that would be me and my two boys." As we walked around the side of the house and out the back toward the treehouse, the conversation turned on bureaucratic words like, "council regulations," "liability insurance," "litigation," and so on. The more he talked, the more I wanted him to leave. We both stood at the bottom of the tree, looking up.

"Well it's certainly a great treehouse, one of the best I've ever seen," he said.

"Do you have kids?" I asked, searching for the person behind the uniform.

"Yes, three boys, and they would certainly love this!"

"I bet they would," I replied. "Parents come from miles around to let their children enjoy what is a pretty unique experience these days. There must be some way of keeping it?"

"Look, it's a great treehouse, but I'm only doing my job. I'm sorry, but the treehouse will have to come down. It's on council land and it's not an approved structure. You will soon get a letter in the mail, and after that you will have three weeks to comply. I know it's not what you wanted to hear, but I'm sure you understand," and with that he walked off.

What was I meant to understand? All I knew was that we had a perfectly good treehouse that did nothing but bring hours of fun and laughter to the lives of many children and now the council wanted me to smash it down. I guess the uniform was too strong for the man who hid inside it.

My thoughts turned to the boys. What was I to tell them? The more I thought about it, the more I realised that nothing was going to make sense. How do you explain to children that the treehouse they built with their dad, the wonderland they shared with their friends and the place they called their second home, now had to be ripped apart, thrown to the ground and taken away, never to be seen again? That sinking feeling began to get worse.

After returning home from school, the boys took the news as expected. Shock turned to confusion, confusion turned to sadness, and lots of tears followed.

"But how could you let this happen?" they asked. "It's our treehouse, Dad. Why don't you stop them?"

As young boys growing up, they had always looked to me to make sure their world was okay. I had an answer for everything. I was their dad and nothing in this world was out of my control. I usually had a way of making things turn out okay. That's what dads are meant to do. But not this time. This time, I had been exposed. Were they beginning to see some holes in my armour? How could I let this happen? As a father, I had never felt so helpless.

When the letter arrived in the mail, my sadness, too, turned to anger. Was I going to let this go without a fight? Was I simply meant to acquiesce to the council's rules and regulations without so much as a peep? What would my boys think? The more I thought about it, the more fired up I became. It didn't make sense. Why did something as innocent as a treehouse, a symbol of everything good in the world today, have to be destroyed? In every way imaginable, it was a life-affirming experience that every child so desperately required and yet the rules that govern the way we live and behave were now demanding that this place be smashed down.

It was wrong. In fact, it was more than wrong, it was an injustice inflicted upon our children by a world gone mad.

I decided then and there to let the world know.

Having spent twenty years working in the media, I had a good understanding of how it all worked. If an injustice was being done, I wanted to make sure as many people as possible knew about it. But more important to me, I wanted to see if anyone else cared. I called the boys together and they climbed up into the tree. Capturing their looks of despair, I took a photo that I emailed to the local newspaper, accompanied by a letter explaining the imminent demise of a choice treehouse. As I expected, the local newspaper was interested in the story—about a fight between a father, the local council, and a treehouse. The story made page three of the local rag. The best was yet to come.

I decided to write to a few local councillors to see what kind of support I might be able to drum up for the tree house. I titled the letter, "In Search of a Courageous Councillor." I sent out the invitation to quite a few of the local constituents, but only one replied. A brief meeting with him at the base of the treehouse brought the usual rhetoric.

"It's a great treehouse. I see your point. But unfortunately, my hands are tied!"

Nothing courageous about that, I thought.

Another week passed, and one day while pottering around in the shed, I heard the rattling of a truck go past my back fence. I watched as a young guy and girl from the local council, dressed in khaki uniforms, got out and began admiring the treehouse. The young lass took a keen interest in the structure. She took out a small camera and began walking around the base, taking photos. I watched from a distance, intrigued by what was going on. The woman turned, walked back to the truck, and put the camera on the front seat. She walked around to the back of the truck where the guy was busy reaching under the tarpaulin for what appeared to be some tools. To my surprise, he pulled out a long sledgehammer and passed a saw to his female colleague. As they approached the tree house, I realised that it was time for me to quickly show my face.

"Hi there!" I yelled, as I briskly walked toward them. From the look on their faces, they were obviously surprised to see me.

"What do you think of my treehouse?" I asked.

"I love it," said the young lady. "I even took a photo of it."

"Yes I saw. So what's the hammer and saw for?" The mood suddenly changed as she looked toward her male companion.

"Well, we've been given instructions to knock it down," she said. As the young lady kept talking, I soon found out that neither was very happy about the assigned task. They told me they were actually part of the environmental unit and were quite upset about being dragged in to knock down a treehouse. Having now seen how wonderful it was and with my presence, they became nervous about what to do next.

"Why would you knock down a perfectly good treehouse that brings so much joy to the local children?" I asked.

"I don't think I can!" she replied. And with that, she decided to call her boss. From the tone of the conversation, I could tell her boss wasn't happy with her reluctance to follow his orders.

"No I won't!" she yelled down the phone, hung up, got in the truck and drove off.

First victory for the treehouse, I thought. But the battle had just begun.

Sitting in my office later that week, my phone rang and a familiar voice came on the other end.

"Hi Darrell, how are you today?" It was a producer from the local TV news program *Today Tonight*. As freelance cameraman, I had shot many stories for them in the past. This time, I was the story!

"I believe you're having a bit of trouble with the local council?" she said with a smile in her voice. Battles between treehouses and local councils were not unusual, and often made for good television. Having spotted the photo of my treehouse in the local paper, they were keen to run a story. I agreed to an interview and we arranged a time later that week to meet up.

In the meantime, two local radio stations had also got wind of the "David and Goliath story" (as they liked to describe it) from an article that had now shown up in The West Australian, Perth's biggest newspaper. Apparently The West also saw the story in the local rag and decided to run their own story on page three. I was now scheduled for two radio interviews: one for the ABC and the other for 6PR, as well as a national TV story. Certainly, the growing publicity about the treehouse was becoming a concern for the local council. Public support for the treehouse was overwhelming, and the council knew it. They wanted the story to go away in a hurry.

Over the next couple of weeks, I engaged the local council on radio and TV. We debated the legitimacy of the treehouse on many fronts. In the back of my mind, I think I knew that ultimately the treehouse would be pulled down. I was just buying time to give as many kids as possible the chance to come and experience it. But I was also trying to shine a light on the kind of society we were now becoming. Finally a decision was made and the council informed me that the treehouse was to be pulled down. The following day I made a sign and attached it to the base of the tree:

BEFORE YOU TEAR THIS TREE HOUSE DOWN...

Try and imagine this:

In years from now, a small boy will ask his grandfather: "Please tell me one more time Grandpa, tell me the story about those magical, mystical things called treehouses. What were they like?"

I couldn't imagine a sadder, lonelier world for children to grow up in than that.

If you choose to participate in the destruction of this treehouse, then there's really no hope for us anymore.

Remember that you are a human being with a conscience before you were ever an employee of a city or shire.

"Our lives begin to end the moment we remain silent about things that matter."

—Martin Luther King

With the boys at school, Jules and I were home going about our business when once again, I heard a truck pull up outside my back gate. This time, a young man had arrived with a security guard. He got out, pulled out a large sledgehammer and began to rope off a ten-meter area around the base of the tree house with "do not enter" tape. I yelled out to Jules that this looked like the end for the treehouse. We both rushed out the back and tried to plead with the young lad not to smash it down. His response angered both of us.

"These treehouses are a danger to kids, mate!" he yelled. "Stay back because I'm about to knock it down."

Jules walked straight under the tape, raced past the security guard, and reached the base of the treehouse. She had watched her two young boys help their dad proudly build this treehouse. She had looked on as they climbed up and pretended to be pirates and adventurers. This treehouse had played a wonderful part in her boys' growing into young men. She had invested much of her heart into this experience and to her it meant much more than just a treehouse.

"You're not smashing it down!" she yelled, and jumped in front of the tree, while I climbed up into the branches. The young guy didn't raise an eyebrow. He picked up his sledgehammer and took a swipe at the tree house with us in it!

"Whoa, whoa!! Stop!" The security guy immediately ran over. "Sorry mate, but you can't take a swipe at the treehouse with them in it. Let me call my boss."

Jules rang her mum and dad, who lived around the corner. They decided to come and join in the fight, as did our next door neighbours, including an 80-year-old grandmother. As a group started to gather under the treehouse, we were eventually joined by two members from the local council, two security guards, and about a dozen police officers with handcuffs, batons, and a police wagon. I guess those grandmothers can really look threatening.

I climbed out of the tree and spoke to the group.

"You know, somewhere out there in the community, there's probably a real crime being committed. And yet we have a dozen police officers here to make sure a boys' treehouse gets smashed down. Does anyone see what's wrong with this picture?"

Though many of the officials present seemed sympathetic to the cause, their response was the usual, "We're just doing our job." We were given an ultimatum: either move away from the tree house or be carted off to the local police station. Reluctantly, we moved away, but not before my final address to the gathering:

"None of you can go home tonight and say you did the right thing. The best you can do is say that you did what you were told. All of you have a conscience that transcends what you do for a living. If you continue to smash down treehouses, you'd better build bigger prisons…because you're going to need them. Treehouses allow children to engage in playful interaction, a vital part of the socialisation of their childhood. If you knock down this treehouse, you send a message to children that they should go back to the isolation of their own homes and their Internet chat rooms, even perhaps violent video games. Is that the kind of community you were hoping for when you signed up for your position?"

My voice was met with silence as the inevitability of the situation unfolded.

As we moved away from the tree house, everyone else left. Jules couldn't face what was about to happen and retreated back to our home, comforted by her mum and dad. I remained, however, and painfully watched as the young guy climbed up into the treehouse and began to systematically smash it to pieces. He tore the dinosaurs out and threw them to the ground. Ripped out the telescope and cut down the ropes. With every smash of the hammer, a piece of my heart took a hit. Every part of it torn down and dumped at my back gate.

When he finally drove away, I was left looking up at a vacant tree. I tried hard to make sense of it all. How could this still happen in today's world? How did society get to this point? I struggled with the questions running through my head. There were no winners here today. All I could hear were the words of Cody and Taylor and the looks on their little faces: "Daddy, promise us you won't let them tear down our tree house." What was I to tell them? I felt I had betrayed them as a dad. I was meant to be their answer to life's problems. I was their best bet. As a tear ran down my face, I remember thinking, *The saddest thing about today is that I don't have the answer that they deserve.*

Though many years have passed since that day, people still walk past and ask us about the famous treehouse. Though the boys are now much older, the memories of that magical place will always remain a special and vital part of their unfolding into fine young men. Maybe one day, many years from now, they, too, will build a treehouse with their own children.

Sometimes in the evenings when I sit out the back in my yard and I look over to the vacant tree, I can still hear the voices of my two little boys climbing, laughing and playing with their dad—a memory no one can ever tear down.

11

THOSE TEENAGE YEARS

Have you ever looked at your kids and thought, *Wow! How did they grow up so fast?"* It's like you blinked and missed a few years. It's funny how time creeps up on you. As parents, we sometimes wish our kids could stay little forever.

When our boys were about four and five, we would take them to huge shopping malls. Jules would dress them up in their little overalls. Seeing them so innocent and looking so cute brought me so much joy. As I walked them through the shopping centre, their eyes would open wide with excitement, as their little legs ran from shop to shop. Now that they could walk, I didn't feel the need to put them in a stroller.

For me, being with my children was about eye contact and facial recognition. As toddlers, children become highly attuned to their parents' facial expressions. They constantly look to us to see how we react to the changing environment. Ever notice when a stranger walks into the room, the first thing a toddler will do is look to his or her parents to see the reaction on their faces? If you're smiling, then you're telling them the world is still okay, this person is a friend.

As the boys skipped along at the shopping mall, they would constantly look back to me to see how far they could venture. Sometimes I would stop, and when they lost eye contact with me (I could still see them) almost instantly I'd see concern cross their faces as they looked for me in the crowd. If you leave a child alone too long, panic sets in.

When I was about four years old, I got lost in a shopping centre. It scared the hell out me. I wondered if my parents would ever find me again in this big, wide, and crowded world. Of course, I never let it get that far with my boys. I always kept a keen eye on them. At the same time, I loved their spirit and sense of adventure. I loved seeing them both run off, then turn back to see me give them that "get back here!" look, then see them scuttle back into my arms, laughing and giggling.

I wanted them to learn this life lesson as early as possible: "Go forth on your journey, boys. Adventure far and wide. Set off on the hero's journey, and fight the good fight. Slay the dragons and save the princess. But always remember, there's a safe home waiting for you whenever you choose to return."

Loving and attentive dads push the boundaries of their boys' safety. They lead them to the edge of danger, then share with them the wisdom, courage, and resources to handle things. And when life gets too much, Dad is waiting with strong open arms to provide a trusting place for them to return to—to gather their thoughts, soothe their emotions, release their tears, heal their scars, and gather their strength for the next stage of their life.

I remember Cody walking into the kitchen one morning to make breakfast. As he stood next to me, I realised I no longer had to look down to meet his eyes. At fourteen, he had already reached my height. His voice had dropped and his feet were now bigger than mine. He was eating more than me at meal times, and could definitely outrun me in a race. Where was my "Little Boo" who used to run to my arms and ask, "Daddy, where's my blanky and dumb-dumb?"

Every age provides us with different experiences. As my boys grew into teenagers, I noticed that our conversations became more and more one-sided:

"How was your day, son?"

"Good."

"What was the best part?"

"Sport."

"Have you got much homework?"

"A bit."

When they were little, I would come home from work and be bombarded with questions. Now it's me doing all the asking. Looking back, I really miss those days. It was kind of nice to be in demand. Even though at the time I sometimes felt like I wanted a break, there was something very special about being the centre of their world—the one with all the answers. The one who's attention they demanded.

The time had come to give them space.

As the boys grew into teenagers, I could see that the game had changed, once again. Parenting is like that. It's a dynamic, ever-changing process. Just when you get comfortable with the way things are, someone changes the rules.

When boys stop talking to us as much as they used to, mums seem to find it particularly difficult. Mothers want to talk to their boys—a lot. They want to know what they're thinking, where they are going, and who they're hanging out with. I'm not suggesting this isn't a good thing, I'm simply suggesting you might not get much of a response. It's normal for teenage boys to pull away from their parents and move toward their peer groups.

During the teen years, the world becomes a strangely mysterious place, and teens want to spend their time trying to find their place in it. They explore, follow their adventurous spirit, experiment with the current trends among their peers, struggle with emotional storms—always trying to find their own identity. The hard part for us is that this new identity is separate from their parents'. Boys create and adopt their own language in the schoolyard, on Facebook, and at sports training. They like to spend a lot of time chatting online. Today, teens take social media for granted, the way previous generations took the radio or the postman for granted.

Like most parents, I felt that the "digital invasion" threatened my relationship with my kids. I don't have a problem with my boys having secrets. I am happy for them to be independent. I don't want to monitor their Facebook page or ask them too much about what they did at a party. I read a lot about cyber-safety and hear experts telling parents to get a "Net-nanny" to constantly monitor your children's online activity. For some parents, this might be the way to go, I guess we approached it a little differently.

If you have teenage boys, they have probably seen things by age eleven that you didn't know about until your mid-twenties.

That's the brave new world we live in, and as parents, we shouldn't be surprised. Of course, we did monitor the boys' laptop use earlier on, and didn't allow them onto Facebook until they were thirteen. But trying to police their access to the Internet would not only have been almost impossible, it just didn't make sense.

We took a more holistic approach to things. Rather than spending most of our energy trying to stop them from viewing inappropriate material, we spoke to the boys openly about the kind of material they were likely to be exposed to. We asked them how they felt about these things and how it fit into their lives. We spoke about values, relationships, respect, and sex. Nothing became taboo; anything was on the table.

These became important conversations at dinnertime when we turned off the TV and put the digital screens away. We created a space where the boys knew they could talk to us about anything. Having an uncle who was gay (my half-brother) invited us to speak openly about our sexuality. Living in a three-bedroom house with one shared bathroom meant we all became comfortable with the naked body. There was nothing to hide, and of course we always added humour to those inevitable embarrassing moments. At the end of the day, this helped prepare the boys for the kinds of things they would be exposed to online.

We wanted to give them a context for the blizzard of information available through the Web. If the boys knew what to do with whatever they were viewing, and how it related to their own values, we were confident they would work their way through the maze of inappropriate material they would eventually stumble across online.

Rather than make a big deal about things, did our best to remain calm and asked our boys what it meant to them (whatever the significant online "it" happened to be). Like all parents there were also times when we felt over whelmed and struggled to find the right answers. We often found ourselves talking the next morning about how we could have handled a situation better. I guess that's the key, taking time out to reflect on the things that didn't work without going into blame. Something Jules was always better at than me.

We spoke calmly, openly, and curiously about these subjects with our kids as they moved into their teenage years, hoping this would allow them to find the resources within themselves to deal with what they find. Of course, when the boys were still little, prevention was our priority. That is why they never had TVs or other screens in their bedrooms.

We tried to keep everything age-appropriate, and it's always a dance between when to start having the "right conversations" and when to give them more access to private online time.

It all comes back to the relationships you create with your children early on and how strongly you bond with them. The deeper that connection, the more likely they are to take on board those meaningful conversations you have with them. The greater your loving connection is, the more likely they will be to take your advice. That's why it's so important to invest a lot of time into your relationships with your kids when they are young. When life's inevitable defining moments arrive for your kids—when they have to make choices that might mean having to go against the strong influence of their peers—those dinner-table conversations, those warm hugs at night, and the love that kept your connection so strong, will rise to the surface when it matters most.

Sometimes when we are not connected to our kids, we wonder why they go off the rails. We wonder why they stop listening to us, and refuse to do what they are told. If a child isn't invested in a relationship, or doesn't get anything from it, the relationship is fragile. That's when children and teens are most vulnerable to their peer groups, like the gangs who hang around the shopping malls looking for trouble. As much as we might not like to admit it, many teens get more out of their relationships with their peers than with their mum and dad.

Every child is searching for love. If they don't get it at home, they will look for it somewhere else—most often among their peers. Of course, what they get in that case is rarely love. At best, they get a form of connection. They can often find a sense of belonging in their peer group, which serves as a surrogate family where at least they feel accepted. If teens' relationships with their parents turn sour, they often feel drawn to their peer groups, desperate to find the connection they desire. Although it's not love, this sense of belonging is the next best thing. A teenage boy who doesn't feel loved will always be vulnerable to his peer groups. Unfortunately, these groups can often resemble gangs where most of the other boys have also lost their connection with their own parents. Together, they make their own "family." The more they find closeness in this group, the more they usually begin to rebel against their natural family.

Something draws them to these gangs: *a sense of significance*—one of the highest human needs. When a young lad doesn't feel loved at home, he also loses his sense of self-worth. In a gang, he can be persuaded to do things he wouldn't usually do. You hear this a lot when young boys are returned to their parents by the police after a night out with "their gang." We frequently say that our son's behaviour was very "out of character." Attempting to fit in, young boys often take on a new persona, one that makes them fit in more with the gang—one that makes them feel significant.

However, ultimately peer-group connection is always "conditional." As soon as they go against the group, or try to tread a different path, the "rebels" are singled out and bullied. The pain of being rejected forces them to either fall back in line or to search elsewhere for a place to belong. By default, gangs will always be a wounding environment, young boys raising other boys never ends well. Nothing but the unconditional love of a patient, understanding parent or loving adult caregiver can ultimately fix the wounded heart of a young boy.

As our boys begin their teenage years, we must be present in their lives, with strong voices and warm hearts. The voices that surrounded them in their early childhood years are now guiding them into adolescence. As parents, we are required to monitor our conversations. What messages are they are hearing from us?

When our boys were little, Jules and I could have "adult conversations" in their presence that perhaps went over their heads. Now, we have to be careful regarding what we speak about in their company. In particular, we used to try to keep them from hearing about money matters. Like a lot of parents money was sometimes tight for us. Paying the bills some weeks was a struggle; however, we were determined not to let the boys know. Though we didn't argue very often, the times when we did were always about money.

As the boys became teenagers, it became more difficult to hide this reality from them. I'll never forget the time that, after an argument over money, one of the boys turned to me and asked, "Dad, are we poor?" Straightaway, I realised that the boys were now well aware of the conversations we thought we were having in private.

Knowing that our boys could understand our conversations, I began wondering, "Are these 'voices' becoming part of our boys' belief systems?" I didn't want them to grow up thinking that money was difficult to make and that life is always a financial struggle. We explained to them that this was a temporary situation, and that we were confident we could turn things around, that lots of money was on its way to us.

Jules helped put things in perspective. She pointed out that in many ways we were wealthier than many people. We had our health, our friends, and our family. We lived in the most wonderful county in the world, and in one the best cities in that country. We had things that money could never buy, and these made our life rich.

As our boys became teenagers, we knew it was important that they hear the kind of voices inside their heads that would guide them on the right path in the important decisions they would soon be making about their own lives. It's funny, but I began to feel that as the boys were getting older, they were beginning to see my imperfections. From the questions they asked, it became obvious they had noticed not only mistakes I had made in the past, but also ones I make day to day.

On a recent holiday to Bali, the boys noticed how warm and welcoming the Balinese people were. Jules and I reminded our boys to always smile and say "please" and "thank you" for everything. We loved that they noticed the kindnesses constantly offered to them by these caring people. In the evenings, we would walk along the beach and find a different restaurant for dinner. One evening, after ordering our meal, we wondered why it took so long to arrive. Forty minutes had passed, and I was becoming both hungry and frustrated.

When the waiter finally arrived, I angrily asked him why it was taking so long. I rudely tapped my watch and said, "If it's not here in five minutes, we're going to leave!" The waiter seemed upset at my outburst, and quickly left to find out why the order was taking so long. The boys looked at me and suggested that I was way out of line with my comments. They reminded me of how polite the waiter had been and that he didn't deserve to be spoken to like that.

In no time at all, another waiter returned with our tray of food and apologized for the delay, saying they wanted to make sure the food was prepared especially to our liking. I felt terrible and told the boys they were right in saying what they did. I was glad they had taken the higher ground. They could have easily taken my side and joined the chorus of complaint. "Yeah, Dad, let's get out of here!" But they didn't. I had challenged one of their values: kindness and compassion; and even though they loved me dearly, they were wise enough to separate me from my behavior.

They reminded me that I had a higher choice than the one I had just made. In doing so, they showed me what fine young men they were becoming. In that moment, I knew that the voices of their childhood were holding them in good stead, and I found comfort in the knowledge that the world was becoming a better place with them in it.

12

MR. PRESIDENT

It was one of those cold winter nights when most people would have been happy to simply stay rugged up in front of the TV.

"I'm just going down to stick my head in at one of those committee meetings!" I yelled out to Jules.

"Don't do that," she said. "You'll end up the president!"

Growing up, I always had a keen interest in sports. Although I was never athletically gifted, I did think of myself as a good coach. Cody and Taylor both loved playing sports. In fact, like most boys, they loved playing outside in general. When they were still toddlers I bought them a soccer ball, the game I used to play as a boy. However, the strong football culture surrounding us had taken hold, and the soccer ball was soon replaced by "Australian Rules" football as their winter sport. In summer, cricket was the name of the game. Their years were pretty much taken up with these two sports.

When the boys were little, I would often take them to the park and they would have a blast either kicking the ball in the goal or playing cricket in the nets. I knew the importance of this time together, and although the boys enthusiastically focused on playing the sport, I would often bring their attention to a passing flock of galahs or an interesting sunset forming in the distance. It was never just about the sport.

In fact, sometimes we would completely forget about the game. If someone happened to walk by with a puppy, we'd drop everything and run over to check it out. As long as the boys were happy, I was fine to go with the flow. It added more layers to our relationship.

When we got back to playing football or cricket, I would give them my complete attention and guide them through the proper technique of kicking the ball or holding the cricket bat. Their attention spans were short, so I would give them small chunks of concentrated effort at a time, and then allow them to play and enjoy the experience. These short moments of concentration allowed them to get a good technical understanding of each chosen sport. And so it would go: each night we had fun mixed with some strong coaching techniques.

After a while, their "natural ability" shone through effortlessly. I wondered, though, if it was "natural" or a result of a good mix of fun, focused intent and, most important, the "right relationship." Children are very good at noticing their parents' facial expressions. Our boys began to recognise when I was about to teach them something important and that it was time to focus on me. In these moments, I had their undivided attention and would give them the "good oil" on how to hold a football, etc. Then I would hand it over to "play" and the magic would mix it all together.

One evening, a woman came by and stopped to watch the boys play in the cricket nets. After a while, she came over to me and asked how old the boys were. "Six and five," I replied. She said she thought they were handy players for their age and suggested they were just about old enough to join the local kids' cricket club. I thanked her for her suggestion and she slowly moved on. My reaction was mixed. As fathers, we live such busy lives that our time with our boys is very precious. Some guys are lucky to get an hour in the evenings to take their kids to the park before the sun goes down.

I couldn't help thinking to myself, why would I want to bring my boys down to the park and hand them over to another guy to coach while I sat at the sidelines and watched? I know, of course, that dads are always welcome to be involved; however, in those early years, when time together is so precious, being available to play with my kinds was a no brainer. I knew I had so much more to offer in those vital years. Besides, I don't think I have ever seen a coach stop training to watch a flock of birds fly past or run over to a puppy. Those little "extras" are just as important as learning how to hold a cricket bat.

We now know that play is absolutely vital to the brain development of young children. What makes play unique- is being void of any "contest." As soon as we create winners and losers, we stifle that development and often replace it with anxiety that comes from the need to meet certain outcomes. This is why "screen time" is not considered by child developmentalists as play. Natural play defines itself by being free of any outcome.

As a father, I was not getting the boys into a competitive environment too early. Unfortunately, in a lot of places now, spontaneous "free play" in childhood has been systematically replaced by organised activities. All this is age dependent and parents have to individually decide on the right time to hand over their children to competition.

Of course, in the absence of a father, having someone else to coach boys is a wonderful option. But for me, this was a critical time in their lives and I wanted to take a more holistic approach to their development. Sports became a vehicle for me to build my relationship with the boys. In fact, I'm hesitant to even call it "sports." Really it was just *play*. At that age, they don't need a lot of adult interruption. Sometimes they would simply drop the cricket bat and pick up sticks to have a sword fight. This was all okay. When they were ready to learn a bit more about cricket, they would always let me know. As they got older, they began to want more directed involvement from me. The boys' natural competitive nature became more apparent as they tried to hit the ball harder or bowl it faster than their brother.

Later on, both of my boys grew into talented sportsmen. Although they started in their respective sports later than most, they both showed a lot of natural ability. Possibly those moments of focused intent coupled with free-spirited play provided fertile ground for their innate abilities to shine through.

In joining the committee, I soon became the junior football manager for the entire club. It was a club that was growing quickly in numbers, and I thoroughly enjoyed working with both the parents and the young boys. My managerial role also included dealing with complaints that came from the local district. I soon found myself having to investigate things such as unruly behaviour on the field, umpire abuse from parents, and out-of-control coaches. My four years as football manager presented me with opportunities to make a lot of friends and certainly tested my communication skills.

They say the worst thing you can ever do as a volunteer is a good job because it usually means they find more things for you to do. Jules had echoed these sentiments that winter night, and sure enough, her prophetic words came true. I was elected the new club president, responsible for six hundred boys, over a thousand parents, twenty coaches, and fourteen committee members.

I felt humbled by the privilege of leading the club, and had it not been for the amazing group of men and women around me, taking on that role would have been even more daunting. I used to joke at the time that I must have been the only president of a football club in Australia who had never played the game, or had never downed a glass of beer. On the surface, my credentials didn't look good. People would often ask me then how I became president of a football club. My response was short: I guess I loved my boys that much.

You see, I had two young boys who loved football, lived and breathed it. As long as my boys' lives were all about football, I wanted to be there, too. As a father, I kept finding ways to be a part of their lives. I know a lot of coaches who feel the same way. They love coaching football because it gives them the opportunity not only to be in their own sons' lives, but also the lives of their sons' friends. I simply looked for the best way I could contribute to both.

Because I hadn't come from a footballing background, I looked at the football environment with different eyes. I started thinking more about the things we could do off, as well as on, the field. In my first year as football manager, I decided to have an end-of-year debriefing session with all the coaches. Much of the discussion hinged on the balance of the teams, the boys' skill level, and interpretations of the rules. These were important topics for the coaches. Because I didn't have a football background, I was more than happy to oversee and facilitate the discussion rather than try to contribute any football knowledge.

However, at the end of the meeting, I made an observation. I told them that, as football coaches, their main task was to help our boys develop into young footballers. At the same time, I noted that perhaps they had an even bigger responsibility.

I suggested that the world can sometimes be a lonely and confusing place for young boys. When they turn up for football training, we never really know what's going on in their lives at home. For some of these boys, the two hours a week they spend with their coach might be the only time all week they have a strong male role model. All it takes is one conversation to change a boy's life. Sometimes, it could be something as simple as a wink of the eye or a pat on the head, letting a young boy know everything is okay, he's going to be all right. My invitation to the coaches was to think of themselves as not only football trainers, but more as life coaches. "Yes, it's good to develop these boys into young footballers," I said, "but let's not miss the opportunity to help them to develop into well-balanced young men as well."

The football coaches at our club knew exactly what I was taking about. In fact, many of them did this already. Sometimes, having these kind of conversations around other guys can start to break down cultural barriers, so that they, too, begin to open up and talk about things close to their hearts. I have found that when someone takes the initiative to speak first, the atmosphere in the room softens and allows the conversation to go deeper.

I think a lot of men can remember a time in their childhood when the world seemed a little crazy. At times like that, young children would love to have someone give them a smile, a hug, or just sit down for a chat and ask them how their life is at home, at school, and with their friends. I suspect the coaches responded so positively to my comments and observations because I reminded them of what it was like to be a young boy.

I don't think such words were expected at a coaches meeting, but they were certainly well received. I wanted to start changing the language used around the club. I started to think about how junior football clubs presented great opportunities to reach out to young boys in ways that perhaps their parents (at least some of them) hadn't thought of before.

Sometimes we think that great change comes only from the top down, that we need governments to make the changes required for a society to move forward. However, history tells us that's not the case. I always remember the words, "When the people are ready to lead, our leaders will be ready to follow." I viewed junior football clubs as opportunities for grassroots change—reaching out to young boys struggling in today's fast-changing world.

In the city where I lived, the "absent father" syndrome was definitely a sign of the times. Perth was very much a FIFO city—where, each week, thousands of fathers would "fly in and fly out" to mine sites across the country. Many of these guys would work three weeks away, then spend one week at home. Not surprisingly, the FIFO schedule had an unfortunate effect on families. Many left-behind mothers struggled every month to raise children on their own. The toll of absenteeism went beyond individual families into society at large.

Many Australian men also work longer hours than their counterparts in nearly all other developed countries. Gone before breakfast and home late for dinner, these fathers looked and felt absent to their children. To top it all off, divorce rates are at an all-time high and many dads struggle to simply get access to their kids.

I want to emphasise here that I don't blame any fathers that fall under these categories. After all, they are trying hard to meet the financial commitments of living in one of the most expensive cities in the world. And they pay the price in more ways than one. Believe me, I encounter this challenge daily. I feel for fathers who long to spend more time with their kids. However, we can't ignore the fact that boys are in desperate need of their fathers—perhaps now more than ever before.

As I looked around the football club, I realised that our junior football club had within its walls all the ingredients for a young boy to thrive in society. With no prior experience in junior-level football, my background in understanding boys allowed me to take a holistic view of how a football club could position itself in the community.

I wanted to further pursue these ideas about raising children, but the time commitment of being club president got in the way. I decided to step down and take up a less-demanding senior role on the committee. This allowed me to focus more on how we could begin to change the culture of the club and start implementing some key ideas.

To test the waters, I put together a PowerPoint presentation titled "Welcome to Junior Football!" for all parents new to the sport. I discussed my ideas with the committee and they got right behind the concept. We set a date for the event, and invited the seventy or so parents who had young boys starting their first year of junior football.

Being a weeknight, thirty or so parents showed up. I know how hard it can be to make time, given all the demands made on parents these days. I was happy with the group that came, and let them know that they would have to be the ambassadors of the evening's information and pass it along to parents who couldn't make it that night.

I began the presentation by talking about the mandatory rules and bylaws for junior football. We touched on tackling, crowd behaviour, and umpire abuse. I spoke about parents' game-day duties: goal umpiring, bringing the oranges, serving as water runners, and umpire mentors. We went on to a Q&A session, in which I told the assembled parents that the part of the presentation they had expected was over. Now I wanted to talk about something they probably weren't expecting.

I clicked to the next slide: "What's the difference between a good football club and a great football club?" I explained that, in my view, the difference depended on the culture created by the club. In turn, the club's culture is created by the stories people tell. I suggested that we could begin to tell a story about our club to help it become a great club.

Roughly, here's the story I told:

Sometimes, the world can be very confusing and lonely for young boys. It is a very different place from the one their parents grew up in. Today's children grow up in a digital world, the likes of which no generation has ever experienced before. The massive advances in technology have radically changed the landscape of family life. Many would agree that these advances have added a tremendous amount of positives to our daily lives. However, for many reasons, our young boys have become particularly vulnerable to these changing times. Kids today do most of their communicating over the internet, constantly using Facebook and other social media to stay connected. Unfortunately, without the wisdom that comes with age, the Web can often be a particularly wounding environment. In the absence of parents, youngsters look to each other for guidance. However, boys raising other boys never ends well. Family relationships are hierarchical by nature, and boys need this structure.

Apparently the problem isn't so much what our children are doing online; the greater damage occurs because of what is lost when the internet replaces face-to-face family relationships. As our boys' environment changes, we must learn to respond to these changes. The same applies to our football club, I said.

I expressed that I had noticed three vital areas where young boys' lives are now under attack.

1) *The Warrior*

Deep down, all young boys have a warrior inside, and nothing brings this out better than a good healthy amount of physical rough and tumble. Boys always compare themselves to their peers and try to measure up. "How strong are you? Well let's see how strong." They love to compete in battles of strength and endurance; many of their games create winners and losers. They need to challenge themselves in order to find their own strengths and weaknesses, and to identify these in their opponents. When two boys line up against each other on the football field, they ready themselves for battle. You see them shoulder-to-shoulder pushing and shoving, already testing their opponents.

As they transition from boyhood to young adult, a natural and healthy process, boys constantly look for circumstances that allow the warrior within to show himself.

2) Male Role Models

All boys desperately require a strong male role model. I'm not suggesting for a minute there aren't many wonderful single mothers out there who do an amazing job raising their boys. But nature has hardwired boys to react specifically to the strong men in their lives. Boys need men who model qualities and values such as courage, integrity, strength, and nobility. They look to the men in their lives for ways to control aggression and focus it with intent toward noble pursuits. Aggression in boys isn't a bad thing; it simply needs context. All ancient cultures knew the crucial role that men were meant to play in boys' lives as they journeyed into manhood.

3) Family

All boys require a family. They need a place to belong. They need a bigger story than just themselves. Family gives them something to stand up for and defend. It brings out both the protector and provider instincts in young boys. Most important, it provides them with a place to call home.

I went on to express to the parents that if a boy gets too distracted by the digital world at a time in his life when nature intended for these qualities to arise, his biological and psychosocial development may drift off kilter. If this happens, he would likely not be well prepared for the world ahead.

Today, junior sporting clubs often substitute for family and strong male role models, filling that void for many young boys. Unintentionally, the clubs often provide an environment for the warrior to play out, as well as offer strong male role models and a family to belong to. If the clubs deliberately and intentionally focused on providing these, I told the parents, I believed we could deliver so much more to our young boys.

Football clubs can often be alpha-male driven environments where the language is all about "manning up" and "growing some balls." Football coaches look for and praise the tough, unforgiving boys in the group who "go hard" and "attack the ball." There's little room for wimps or mommy's boys. I agree that on the battlefield called "a football oval," these qualities will position boys for the tough battles ahead. However, once the boys come off the field, we often struggle with a language to support the other aspects of who they are.

To demonstrate my point to the mums and dads, I presented a slide with a photograph I had taken of my oldest boy, Cody, as a thirteen-year-old playing football. The close-up shot captured him at the moment just after he had kicked a goal to put his team ahead in the dying minutes of the game. His clenched fist, raised in the air as he leapt from the ground and screamed a victory howl at his opponents, underscored the moment of triumph. The warrior inside him had arisen, and the battlefield was his for the taking. I've little doubt that any dad would be just as proud of such a photo, which could easily adorn the wall of any club changing room.

Next, for contrast and to make my main point, I showed them a photograph I had taken of Cody a mere three hours later on that same Sunday. Dressed in a Munchkin outfit, Cody looked nothing like a football hero or warrior. He was one of only two boys in his school year who had auditioned as a dancer for a part in the musical *The Wizard of Oz* at his high school. On stage, the football warrior looked completely vulnerable. No longer on the battlefield, he was very much in touch with another expression of his masculinity.

Music and dance have long been expressions of great warriors and an integral part of a boy's journey into manhood. Acknowledging the yin that balances the yang in every boy might be okay for a high school musical…but at a football club? Such talk would probably be met with scowls of disapproval and incomprehension.

My point was this: Healthy boys grow up willing and able to express *all* of who they are—and this includes not only the Warrior archetype, but also the archetype of Poet or Artist.

Football clubs do provide a strong male environment that serves a vital part of a boy's upbringing. However, we also need to create a language that supports our boys when they come off the field. If we reward them only when they "man up," who are they when they "man down"? As football coaches, managers, committee members, and concerned parents, I summarised, perhaps we need to encourage our boys to balance their football life with these other qualities. As role models for our boys, we need to make sure we engage them in what I call "conversations of the heart," and provide space for them to step into this aspect of their being, without judgment.

In far too many cases, today's generation of fathers have become somewhat emotionally unavailable to boys. Having been raised by men who came through a war-torn world, most of us were told that "boys don't cry." We were taught to bury our feelings inside. As a result, many boys today suffer from depression or some sort of mental illness. The malady is systemic. Modern society lacks an adequate language that allows boys to speak up about the pain in their hearts. And this concerns me deeply.

I'm not suggesting that football clubs should become venues for practicing any kind of developmental psychology. I'm simply suggesting that, as fathers, we need to lead the way in how we show up in our boys' lives. If we don't have a way of expressing ourselves, there will be no hope for our sons. Right now, our boys need us more than ever, and they watch us closely in order to work out how best to behave.

In giving these presentations, I hope to find an audience of men who otherwise might not hear these kinds of conversations. Working in this area, the biggest challenge I have faced has turned out to be getting other *guys* to show up in the audience. By addressing them at a football club, they show up unprepared for the information. The set and setting encourages them to relax and be more open-minded. Fortunately, they always seem so pleased and relieved that someone has raised this topic of conversation.

The more men begin to speak out about matters of the heart, the more we will normalise the experience and begin to turn things around in society.

Junior football clubs provide a rare vehicle for young boys to experience all three important factors for growing up: expressing their inner warrior, having healthy male role models, and feeling part of a substitute family. Currently, a huge tug-of-war exists between the "virtual world" of digital screens and the real world of nature and social interaction. For the sake of our boys, it's a battle we have to win. I am absolutely convinced that if we stay ahead of these changes and create junior sporting environments that allow for the Warrior to come through, provide a loving and nurturing environment, and produce strong male role models that embrace all aspects of our boys, they will put aside those glowing screens in a heartbeat, and run with open arms to their fathers for hints on how to become well balanced young men.

13

A NEED TO KNOW

I mentioned earlier that I wasn't a child psychologist and that I don't have any formal academic training. Although this is true, it isn't the whole truth. In the years leading up to becoming a dad, I became extremely interested in raising children, with a particular interest in early childhood development. I began reading every book I could get my hands on. I looked closely at attachment theory and effect that the environment has on pregnancy and the early years of a child's life.

I wanted to make sure that Jules and I created the best environment we could for our boys. I studied the work of people like Joseph Chilton Pearce, author of *Magical Child*, and *The Biology of Transcendence*. I was fascinated by his research into how a baby's brain structures are greatly affected by its external environment. I ordered his DVDs and listened to more than twenty hours of lectures he gave to early childhood professionals in the U.S.

I also studied the work of Dr. Bruce Lipton, Pam Leo, Meg Meager, Dr. Gabor Matte, Dr. Gordon Neufeld, and many more.

I began collecting all sorts of ground-breaking and cutting-edge information.

I began attending as many workshops as I could, and at one point took a group of 20 people to Melbourne to spend a weekend with Dr. Bruce Lipton, a man I admired and whose work I had been showing and discussing with audiences in Perth. Years earlier I started running information evenings where I would show cutting edge documentaries and facilitate a discussion afterwards. I created a website called www.awakeningevents.net.au where I still to this day advertise my events. They became so popular that I would often get up to 200 people along to an evening.

I met with Bruce Lipton on a number of occasions and showed his ground breaking documentary *Nature, Nurture and the Power of Love* to groups of people around town. Both Dr. Lipton and Joseph Chilton Pearce expressed a wonderful synergy in their work, and it made a big impact on how Jules and I prepared our home environment for our boys.

As the internet took hold, I moved away from reading and started watching hours of talks online by professionals from around the world. Here I found the work of Dr. Gordon Neufeld, arguably Canada's leading developmental psychologist and a leading expert on parenting in today's digital world. After watching hours of his talks online, I applied for membership at his online academy, The Neufeld Institute, and studied modules.

Around the same time, I became deeply interested in NLP (Neuro-Linguistic Programming). After spending four days with Tony Robbins—one of the world's leading motivators—at his "Unleash the Power Within" seminar, I became fascinated with his ability to work with people's limiting beliefs and empower them to make massive changes in their lives. After returning from Sydney and discovering he was trained in NLP, I signed up for a week-long NLP practitioner course with a visiting American trainer, Gary de Rodríguez, a man who was to become not only my trainer and mentor but a very close and dear friend.

Gary taught me about the power of language and how words had a direct impact on the sub-conscious mind. He instructed us in processes we could use to change limiting beliefs that had been handed to us as children and to replace them with new beliefs about who we were, beliefs that could catapult us forward in life. Before I met Gary, one of my greatest fears was public speaking. After training with him for two years, I became a powerful presenter, running my own events and talking to audiences of two hundred people at a time.

Gary trained me to be a master practitioner, and I began working with a small group of clients while still working as a freelance cameraman. I found it to be an interesting mix, two vastly different aspects of my life that I was able to keep separate for some time. After reading as much as I could about NLP, I decided to see if the two creators of this fascinating body of work were still around. NLP was created by two very clever individuals, John Grinder and Richard Bandler. After a quick Google search, I discovered not only were they still around but that John was still running training courses around the world.

I managed to persuade Jules it was important for me to attend his four-day workshop in London. While she stayed at home on mum duties, I booked a flight to London to meet up with John in what was to be a life-changing event. Of all the people I had ever trained with over the years, John Grinder was by far the most incredible to watch.

Neuro-linguistic Programming was based on the work of three of the greatest therapists in the world at the time: Virginia Satir, a family therapist; Fritz Pearls, a gestalt therapist; and Milton Erickson, arguably one of the greatest hypnotherapists of all time. John and his partner, Richard, spent many years in the '70s sitting with all three therapists, watching their every move, trying to find out what exactly it was that made them so incredibly effective in creating change in their clients. They would spend hours together debriefing what they had witnessed. Finally, out of all this research, came the tools and techniques now known around the world as NLP.

I arrived in London on a cold morning and without much sleep. The seminar with John was to begin that evening, and after getting a few hours' sleep in the afternoon, I was tremendously excited about meeting with this man about whom I had read so much. I arrived early at the venue, a function room in a nice hotel in the heart of London.

I sat in the middle of the room so I could get a good feel not only for John but for the audience as well. People had come from all over the world to attend, but surprisingly I was the only one from Australia. The moment John entered the room, he immediately grabbed everyone's attention. As the room went quiet, we waited with bated breath for him to start. A soft-spoken man, he took great interest in his audience, and as the master of non-verbal communication, he read his audience incredibly well. He told us that *how* people speak tells you much more than what they actually say.

He spent that first evening simply asking questions about why participants had come and what they wanted to discover, as well as offering answers to their questions. Being a master communicator, however, John never simply gave a straight answer to any question. He believed the most powerful type of learning is "emergent"—when answers are discovered from within, rather than simply being handed out. John knew that most of the time the question asked often wasn't the real issue. John always tried to find out what was underneath.

John Grinder mentioned that he greatly admired the work of Milton Erickson. Erickson was a storyteller and a believer in the ability of stories to create massive change in people. Stories are powerful because they have the ability to bypass the conscious, analytical mind. Erickson knew that when his clients presented him with a problem they faced, they had a conscious awareness of what that problem was. He knew, however, that the problem had roots hidden deeper, in the sub-conscious mind, and that this was where the work had to be done. Rather than simply address the problem presented, Erickson would begin to tell a story that seemed completely unrelated to the client's immediate concerns.

By telling these somewhat abstract stories, Erickson would bypass his client's conscious mind. Erickson would embed powerful hidden messages within these stories, usually in the form of metaphors. Quite often, clients would leave their appointment feeling a little confused and yet strangely different. For some reason, the problem didn't seem to have as much of a hold on them as when they arrived. Over the next week or two, many of the hidden messages would begin to emerge within his clients. This way, the client would have ownership of the new understanding as the changes would arise from within.

Sitting in the room with John—listening to people ask him questions about their lives, and presenting different challenges they faced—was a wonderful experience. I watched as John would take the person off on a completely different tangent, one seemingly unrelated to the question that was asked. Refusing to answer any question directly, he would often open up one story after another, burying the answers to several questions at a time inside each story while never looking directly at the person the answer was intended for. I watched and listened with many others, trying to keep up with the messages, but eventually gave up and allowed the richness and depth of his knowledge to wash over me. Somehow, when I woke up next morning, it felt like much of his wisdom simply bubbled to the surface.

John had been a professor of linguistics at UCLA in California. He was a wordsmith of the highest order. However, his time spent with Erickson had trained him incredibly well in the art of nonverbal communication. When someone asked John a question, he was more interested in *how* they asked it. He looked at eye patterns, listened to the tonality of their voice, and watched how they emphasized certain words with their hands. He also paid attention to how they were breathing, and to what he called the clients' "micro muscle" movements. This aspect of NLP had also intrigued the great Tony Robbins. Tony's ability to recognise patterns in people's behaviour, especially their non-verbal communication, had allowed him to also become a powerful agent of change around the world.

Before leaving home for London, I had decided to bring my professional video camera. If I was going to travel all the way to London to meet someone who was the best in the world at what they did, I was going to do my best to see if I could interview them. It was a last-minute decision, but one that was to have a big impact on my life. At that time, I happened to be reading a book called *Influence*—about the power to influence people in order to get whatever you want in life. I was reading about the art of reciprocation, and how the best way to get something from someone is to give them something first.

I had decided to bring two gifts to the seminar, one for John and one for his life partner and fellow trainer, Carmen Bostic St Clair. When I arrived at the seminar, I presented John with a "stubby holder" with Australian colloquialisms written around the sides. Because he was a professor of linguistics, I was sure he would appreciate some new phrases to add to his collection. He smiled immediately, grabbed his water bottle, and stuck it straight into the holder, which then sat proudly in front of him for the next four days. Mission accomplished!

Of course, my gifts to John and his partner were unconditional and were given with love. Although I would have been disappointed if he declined the interview, the fact that he enjoyed the gift was itself good enough. In any case, I mentioned to John that I had come all the way from Australia, and that I represented a big NLP following back in Perth. I asked if it would be okay to conduct a short interview with him during my stay, and he agreed.

As a freelance cameraman shooting for programs such as *60 minutes*, I knew how tricky it can be to get a good interview. I had seen many pre-arranged interviews fail from lack of sufficient preparation, so I was determined to do everything I could to make it work. I introduced myself to the hotel concierge and reminded him of the very special guest who was staying at his hotel. I told him I had arranged to interview John Grinder sometime over the next few days, and needed a room I could set up in. Not wanting to let down his important guest, he immediately showed me an available room. However, it was way over the other side of the hotel and I didn't want John to have to walk so far. Instead, I led the concierge back to the function room we were using for the seminar, and asked if it would be okay to use the room next door. He checked to see if it was available, and, to my delight, we were able to lock it in.

Over the next few days, I set the room up each lunchtime, hoping to get John's attention for the interview. However, at each break, John was surrounded by attendees eager to ask questions of the great man. It was difficult to get anywhere near him. However, on the final day, I managed to catch his eye, and he immediately jumped to his feet and walked over to me.

"That's right. You wanted to do an interview?" he said.

I could see the concern on his face, wondering where the hell we were going to go and how long this was going to take to set up. I led him away from the noisy room and into the corridor. "This way," I said. I saw the look of surprise on his face as soon as he entered the room. I had both chairs set evenly apart with the camera on a tripod at one end next to me and a microphone on his chair, which I clipped to his shirt as he took a seat. The light coming from the window lit his face perfectly, and I had organised a carafe of water and glasses so he could loosen his throat. I knew John's time was valuable, and because the lunch break was short, I had to be organised.

Fortunately, the setup was exactly as John liked it. The smile on his face told me we were immediately in rapport—an NLP skill I knew we both understood well. We filled the next 30 minutes with a delightful discussion that I will never forget.

After the four days with John, I had also booked a trip to Leeds in northern England for a week's training in Ericksonian hypnosis. The guy offering the training was a good friend of John's, who also happened to be at the four-day workshop in London. One evening in Leeds, we went for a drink and were chatting about the amazing time we had with John. I mentioned the interview I had done, and he paused, looking at me surprised.

"What do you mean you interviewed him?"

"You know," I said, "with a camera and microphone. I asked him about his new book *Whispering in the Wind*, and we spoke about New Code NLP."

"John Grinder doesn't do interviews," he said.

"Well, he just did one for me," I replied. Though I didn't know it at the time, John had refused many interview requests over the years. After a messy falling out with his long-term NLP partner, Richard Bandler, John had stayed low and had not engaged in any interviews.

Had I known that before I left Australia, I probably would never have taken my camera. However, because I didn't show up with the belief that "John Grinder doesn't do interviews," it didn't get in the way of my outcome. Nor was the expectation of refusal in my voice when I approached John with the request.

When I got back to Australia, I googled John Grinder's name and nowhere could I find a video of John speaking. About a week later, I got a phone call from his Australian sponsors, "Inspiritive," in Sydney, who had somehow found out about the interview. They asked if there was any chance they could get a copy to use on their website. I agreed, on one condition: they must first get John's permission. As a sign of respect for John, I had told him the interview was for my own private purposes and would be shown only to my NLP friends in Perth. A few days later, I got a call from John thanking me for my integrity and to give permission for the interview to be used by his Australian colleagues. The interview went online, and for many years it was the only interview with John Grinder available. In fact, if you're sitting at your computer now or have access to the Internet you can Google "John Grinder in London with Darrell Brown," and still watch it today.

Following the interview and the time we spent together, John asked me to join him in Sydney later that year at what is referred to as "Trainers training". He suggested I would make a good NLP trainer and invited me personally to attend. After much discussion with Jules, I decided to go along. It was a 24-day intensive session where we learned numerous skills focused on creating change within ourselves and the people around us. I noticed many of the attendees were high-powered marketing people who knew that NLP was extremely effective to use in sales. This didn't really interest me at all, as my reasons for being there were a lot more personal. After graduating at the end of the training, many of my fellow participants asked me what I was going to do with my training.

"Are you going back to Perth to do sales training? Run NLP courses?" they inquired. I told them that was not my objective.

"So why are you here?"

I paused and looked them in the eye. "I'm here to see how I can be a better dad." By the looks on their faces, clearly that wasn't the response they were expecting.

My NLP training had a big impact on my life—especially my growing awareness of the power of language. From the day our boys were born, I did my best to only use positive words around them. I knew the effect that negative language had on shaping boys' beliefs—about who they are and what is possible for them in life. As adults, many of our beliefs about ourselves come from the language our parents used to describe us as kids. If you grew up in an environment where you were constantly described as worthless, then you can imagine the effect that could have on your self-belief or "personal paradigm."

Whenever the boys did something we didn't agree with, we always looked at ways of re-framing the event so that the focus was more on what they could do in the future than the problem of what had just happened. A lot of this is common sense, but unless we consciously retrain our mind, it's easy to slip into negative language without even being aware of it. That's what NLP did for me: it reprogrammed my mind so well that whenever I hear anyone using "negative language," something like an alarm bell immediately goes off in my mind.

One of the key insights of NLP is this: The subconscious mind doesn't understand negatives. Imagine, for example, I said to you, "For the next minute I don't want you to think of a pink elephant. Think of anything else; just don't think of a pink elephant." Then, of course, your subconscious mind *will* think of a pink elephant.

Whenever I have spoken about this to audiences, someone always puts their hand up and says: "Not me, I didn't think of a pink elephant."

So I ask them the same question. "Okay, then, what did you think of?"

I get varied responses from, "I didn't think of anything" to, "I was thinking of what I had for lunch, etc."

So then I ask, "How do you know that's not a pink elephant?" You see, in order to *not* think of something, you must first think of what it is you're not meant to think about. Even for just a fleeting moment.

My NLP trainer, Gary, would always say that language is an immediate command for the subconscious mind to "Go there!"

For example, if you said, "Johnny, please don't be a bad boy," Johnny's attention goes straight to, "I'm a bad boy." Contrast that with, "Johnny, can you please be a good boy in future?" In essence, it's the same suggestion, but you're focusing your child's mind on what you want rather than on what you don't. It seems simple, I know, but I tried to imagine the difference in our boys, if we were able to do this throughout their childhood. I wanted to lay the foundations with positive affirming language constantly describing the wonderful young men they are becoming. It's not that we are in denial of things they do that we don't like. It's about always reframing every event towards a positive outcome.

The beliefs we instil in our children often bury themselves so deep they run below the conscious mind. Such unconscious beliefs begin to drive their outlook on life and how they "show up" in the world. The thing about beliefs, of course, is that the older we get, the stronger they become. Our beliefs end up forming our entire identity to the point that, as an adult, our beliefs about ourselves walk into a room about two feet before we do. If we have limiting beliefs about ourselves, they will definitely show up in our language. And if that's happening around our children, then guess what we are likely passing on to them.

The good news is that by simply becoming aware of these beliefs, we can immediately begin to loosen their grip on us. Since our language keeps these beliefs in place, simply becoming aware of our language and training ourselves to make different word choices is a good place to start.

A few months ago, after coming home from work, I walked into the lounge where my two boys were sitting with their laptops. My oldest, Cody, looked at me and said, "Dad, I dumped Sarah today." I reacted immediately and cringed. However, this is what I *said:*

"Cody, if you're trying to tell me you're no longer going out with Sarah, that's fine. I understand at your age that relationships will come and go. But what bothers me is the language you just used. I know Sarah and her mum and dad well and she is a lovely girl. Saying you 'dumped' her does nothing for her at all. Imagine how she would feel if she heard you say that?"

Cody immediately started to back pedal and told me that's just the way the boys speak at school, and he didn't mean it to sound that way. He told me that he and Sarah were still good friends, which I knew would have been the case.

I simply wanted to remind Cody that the choice of words he had used could easily have hurt her feelings, and that, regardless of what the other boys would say, he had a lot of other word choices that he could use in future.

Of course, we all have good and bad days when it comes to raising our kids. On many occasions I have said the wrong things to my boys. This can easily happen, especially with teenagers, who can become quite rebellious and really push your buttons. Often, I will lie on the bed with Jules and say, "You know, I really didn't handle that situation with the boys too well today. I said some things I shouldn't have and I really regret it."

I think we all know those times when we had a better choice than the one we took, but because of anger and frustration we didn't take it. But it's never too late to say you're sorry. On many occasions, I have gone into my boys' room to apologize for things I said or how I acted. Some folks think that saying sorry to your kids is a sign of weakness; on the contrary, it's really one of our greatest strengths.

NLP taught me about the power of language and its ability to shape our children's beliefs. But as much as our kids listen to the words we speak, our actions may very well determine who they become. For example, when they witness us apologizing for our mistakes, they see us at our most vulnerable moments. To be vulnerable in front of your children takes great strength and requires complete trust. They might even take advantage of the moment—but, ultimately, saying sorry demonstrates one of the greatest qualities you can ever have—*humility*.

14

YOU CAN'T TEACH PASSION

My life as a cinematographer was about to take off.

At nineteen, I had been hired as a trainee camera assistant at a state-of-the-art commercial production house—one of the biggest in Australia at the time. I was exactly at the right place at the right time; another one of those so-called "coincidences." Within five years, I had been made senior cameraman, quite a meteoric rise for someone my age.

Throughout my career, I was driven by passion and loved every minute of it. I was soon flying around the country as well as overseas, shooting everything from documentaries to TV commercials. My very first plane trip was a short one-and-a-half hour flight to a town called Kalgoorlie, about 500 kilometres east of Perth. We flew in a fixed-wing light aircraft. To some people this wasn't a big deal; but for me it was extremely exciting.

Growing up, my family never went away on holidays, partly because we didn't have much money, but also because we weren't the kind of family that vacationed together. I didn't think much about it at the time. Only later in life did I realise how sad that was. I remember thinking, "When I get older and become a dad, I will definitely take my kids away as much as possible."

Being a cinematographer gave me an extraordinary window on the world. I was exposed to nearly every occupation imaginable. Some shoots required me to be in one place for weeks on end; others for just a day. I got to see how a lot of the world worked, and I have always been grateful for every experience. In many ways, these experiences helped me in my role as a father.

Finding ways to relate to their children can often be a struggle for parents. As a cameraman, I stayed fresh, always at the cutting edge of news events, new trends, and new technology. I think that the bigger the life you're able to live, the more ways you will be able to find to connect with your kids.

As senior cameraman at a large production studio, I often oversaw inexperienced young men as they came through for a week at a time. They brought with them a varied range of personalities and different levels of enthusiasm for the industry. I would often ask them why they were here and what they were hoping to get out of the week. Some would show a strong interest in whatever shoot we were doing that day; others seemed completely uninterested. I sometimes wondered why they would be wasting such a great opportunity to learn about this fascinating industry.

One day, a young, clean-cut lad named Mark arrived. He followed me around everywhere I went. Every time I set the camera up, he asked me a question. He wanted to know why I was using a certain lens, why I was lighting with different lights. He was in my face the whole time. He had a kind of naive way about him that I actually liked. He wasn't afraid to ask questions, and I could see he was trying to learn as much as he could. It was refreshing, and I wondered why it had taken so long for a young lad with so much enthusiasm to arrive. On the final day of his week with us, I asked him a question, "So Mark, what do you want to do with your life?"

"Be a cameraman just like you!" He snapped back.

"If you could have it tomorrow, would you take it?"

"Yes, definitely," he said. "I would love to!"

I told him to wait there and went upstairs to the production office. I walked over to my boss, Graham, and asked if he was thinking about taking on any new assistants. He asked why I wanted to know, and I said, "Because if you are, then I have the right guy with me downstairs. No need to bother advertising, he's the guy."

"Actually, I was thinking about hiring someone, but not for a few months," my boss replied. However, if you think he's the one, then I'll give him a go."

"Okay, great," I said, "I'll let him know."

As I got to the doorway, my boss called out to me. "But Darrell…he's *your* assistant." I knew what he meant. He was trusting my judgment and, therefore, Mark should come in under my wing. I was more than happy with the arrangement.

I went downstairs and told Mark he could start on Monday. He jumped for joy and told me he couldn't wait to get home to tell his parents. I liked Mark right from the start, I think because he reminded me so much of me. He was young, fresh-faced, and full of enthusiasm.

One thing I had learned about life is that you can teach a boy skills, but you can't teach enthusiasm. That's what *they* have to bring to the party. Give me a kid with passion and drive, and I'll show you someone who is highly teachable.

Mark didn't let me down. Over the next year, he learned everything he could. He never complained, and was always keen to try new things. His future certainly looked bright.

The state-of-the-art building that had been my home for the past six years was owned by an entrepreneurial fellow with a somewhat shaky past. Although we were making money, he had got himself into some other not-so-profitable businesses and the banks began calling in his loans. Ours was his biggest asset and therefore the first to be sold.

Within months, we were all out on the street and the company closed its doors. It wasn't too bad for me because I had enough experience to go freelance—which I did, and started making more money than ever before. But Mark's future was less certain. Eventually, he got a job at a local TV station. Although it wasn't a great place to work, at least it allowed him to remain in the industry.

He phoned me after a few months, disheartened, and said he really missed the creative energy he was used to at our production company. The people he was working with seemed stagnant and lacked the creative buzz that energized our company. At that moment, I had an idea that was to completely change his life.

The TV station where he worked had recently purchased some new camera gear, called a "Steadicam." They used it for the occasional sporting event, but I had recently seen this equipment being used for many other applications. I suggested to Mark that he get proficient with the Steadicam, use it as much as he could, so when it was next needed, he'd be the one to operate it. He liked the idea. He practiced as much as he could for the next few months. Sure enough, one day I got another call.

"Hey Darrell, guess what? You're not going to believe this. An eastern states company is coming over to shoot a kids' TV series here in the west and they want a cameraman who can also use a Steadicam! I've been given the job!"

A skill can be learned, but Mark had to bring his own enthusiasm. And he had plenty. Over the years, I watched his career grow, like mine. He was always in the right place at the right time. Funny that.

Then a production crew from eastern Australia, about to shoot a Seven Networks national TV show "Home and Away," needed a new cameraman—someone who could use a Steadicam. Mark was snapped up by Fox studios, and he began working on high-budget US TV shows. In time, he got to use his talents all over the world. His passion and enthusiasm took him to places he could never have imagined.

Mark often returned to Perth, where his family lived. One night when he was in town, he dropped over for dinner. When I opened the door, he was on the phone and he held up his hand to me as if to say, "Just give me a minute."

A moment later, he entered our home. "Guess who that was?"

"I have no idea," I replied.

Mark explained that he had just finished chatting with Dean Semler—an Academy-award winner for best cinematography on Kevin Costner's *Dancing with Wolves*. Mark was hired to shoot Dean's next film in the U.S. I looked at him, smiling. "You know you've made it, don't you?"

Mark gave me a hug and then looked me in the eye. "Darrell, I've never forgotten what you did for me—giving me my first job. You were the one who believed in me when others didn't. I'll forever be grateful to you for that."

A few years ago, I flew to Sydney to do a shoot. I contacted Mark on Facebook to see if he would be in town and if he wanted to catch up for lunch. He told me that, unfortunately, he was busy working on his latest film... *The Great Gatsby*... with Leonardo Dicaprio. Yes, the young fresh-faced boy from Perth had definitely made it. I guess Mark had picked the right heroes. He followed his passion, never lost enthusiasm, and worked hard at what he believed in.

Robert Bly, a famous American author and storyteller, once said: "Any young boy who isn't currently being admired by an older man is in serious trouble." He was telling the world that every young boy needs someone who believes in him, someone who can hold open a door to their future, presenting them with new possibilities.

If you are a strong man reading this book, I invite you to keep an eye out for these boys. Maybe it's your own son or maybe it's someone else's. Right now, our boys need us more than ever. Let's make sure we're there for them with strong arms, a warm heart, and a guiding voice. You might not pick them, but they may very well pick you.

15

JOIN UP

One of the best parts about being a freelance cameraman is being able to work with so many wonderfully talented people. A great opportunity came my way in the spring of 2008. I must admit the name Monty Roberts didn't mean that much to me when the call-sheet first arrived with the details of my next assignment. I was to spend two days filming at the local equestrian centre filled with a few thousand people and a guy who was going to show them a thing or two about horses.

I was setting up my camera in the middle of the auditorium when an elderly man with a withered face, wearing boots with spurs and a cowboy hat, walked over to me. He reached out his hand and said hello. He had one of those warm smiles that immediately made you feel comfortable. I shook his hand and was surprised by the strength of his grip. "I'm Monty Roberts," he said, "The Horse Whisperer."

Monty was one of those guys you just loved to be around. He was like the grandfather you never had. He spoke with a gentle voice and always looked you in the eye. He felt like one of those people you could never lie to. He was genuinely interested in people and wanted to know their story.

We chatted for a while and immediately hit it off. He asked me if I had kids and I told him I had two little boys. He looked at me with a wry smile and said, "You know, working with wild horses is a bit like working with toddlers." We both had a chuckle, and with that he walked off.

It didn't take me long to figure out why this guy knew horses better then nearly anyone in the world. The next two days with Monty were going to change my life forever.

Remarkably, Monty, now in his late seventies, was still doing close to 300 shows a year. Travelling around the world from country to country, city to city, he was met with a new challenge at every show. Equestrian clubs across the country would invite Monty to perform in front of sell-out crowds and he never disappointed. Before arriving at each centre, his management had already organised the worst of the worst horses to be there with their owners on the day. Horses that had been mistreated, that wouldn't "float," were scared of loud noises, or had never been ridden. Some wouldn't even take a saddle, and others were so damn flighty they would jump at the sight of a small plastic bag.

Over the next two days, I watched and filmed in amazement as he wove his magic with them all. One particular moment, his amazing talent really stood out. A woman walked into the auditorium with her horse in tow and met Monty in the centre of the ring. Behind them, she had a float hooked up to her vehicle. The woman and her horse were introduced to the crowd, and the woman proceeded to tell Monty about the problems she was having with her horse. Apparently, she had been given the horse a few years ago, and ever since it first arrived, it had stubbornly resisted going into the float. The woman explained it would often take up to an hour to get her horse into a float even with three men pulling from the front and two pushing from behind. Sometimes she had to walk the horse for an hour down the road to a neighbour's paddock because it was easier than trying to get it into the float. She said she was at her wits end.

Before Monty got anywhere near the horse, he wanted to know everything about it. He asked about its history and previous owners, how it had been treated, and who looked after it. He asked if there was anything odd or unusual about its behaviour. Finally, when he had gathered all the information, he turned and began to walk over toward the horse. He looked at the horse, then looked back at the woman.

"What's his name?" asked Monty.

"Sundance," she replied.

Sundance was a beautiful chestnut stallion. He was of average size with strong hindquarters; however, he seemed quite agitated and unsettled. Possibly by the large crowd. Perhaps by something deeper.

"How long did you say it took you to get this horse onto a float?" he asked.

"About an hour," she said, and added, "if I have help!"

Monty asked, "What if I said that in the next thirty minutes this horse will enter the float by himself without me even touching him?" The look on the woman's face said it all.

Monty walked over to Sundance and slowly began walking around him. He began telling the audience things about this horse he had deduced purely by observation. He made conclusions about his background from what he had been told and from what he was observing. After working with thousands of horses, Monty could easily recognise patterns of behaviour. He would first tell you what he was thinking, then tell you what Sundance was thinking.

The whole time, he kept walking in circles around the horse, but at no time did he make contact. Sometimes, he spoke to the horse and sometimes he spoke to us, and every now and then he would stop dead in his tracks, as if he was reacting to something the horse did. He would wait for some signal from Sundance, then continue his walk.

"You notice I haven't approached the horse yet?" Monty asked the crowd. "You know why? Because he hasn't asked me to yet. I'm still waiting for the signal." The Horse Whisperer paused. "You see his ears? When his ears drop, that's my invitation." Monty kept moving slowly around the horse.

"Okay, we're just about there, get ready…any second now…there!" And with that, the horse's ears slightly retreated and Monty approached the animal's face. He slowly reached out his right hand and at the same time Sundance raised his nose. With the audience collectively holding their breath, in anticipation of the moment, Monty's hand rested gently on Sundance's head.

"Join up" had occurred.

Monty went on to tell the audience that "join up" is that sacred moment between man and horse when you are finally invited into his world. It's a show of trust and respect that you must always earn. He mentioned that join up is taught to all his trainers and they must be able to demonstrate this with the most difficult of horses before they are allowed into his organization.

"Without join up," said Monty, "nothing but force will work."

I watched as he then put a bridle on Sundance, talking to us and the horse all the time. He continued to let us know what the horse was thinking, and then once again switched to telling us what he was thinking. He explained every movement and action.

Monty then slowly led Sundance toward the float, but for every step Sundance took, Monty would get in under his neck and push him two steps back.

"No, you're not getting in that float," he would say. Then he would again lead him toward the float. "No, no. Back you go. You're not getting in that float."

In what appeared to be some sort of reverse psychology, Monty continued to lead Sundance toward the float, only to then push him back. This back and forth went on for some time. Once again, Monty waited for the signal. By now he had lead the horse straight up the ramp almost into the float, only to once again push him back down the ramp and into the ring.

"Okay," he said to the woman. "Are you ready to watch him walk up into the float by himself?" Monty let go of the bridal and stood with his back to the horse. The entire auditorium fell silent, and then it happened. Sundance walked up and ever so gently nudged his nose against Monty's back.

"That's the signal." Monty then began to walk toward the float with his hands free of any bridle. Sundance followed him up the ramp and walked straight into the float. The stunned crowd applauded loudly. Amazed, the woman acknowledged that had she not seen it, she would never have believed it could happen.

Monty reassured her she would never have trouble with him floating again. Over the next day and a half, Monty continued to work with difficult horses, each with their own unique problems, and yet produced a successful outcome every time. He rode horses that previously wouldn't even take a saddle. He took a horse that was terrified by a small plastic bag and had it walking over a plastic tarpaulin in the space of forty minutes.

At the end of the last day, Monty walked out into the centre of the ring, without any horses, and sat on a stool by himself. A single spotlight focused on him. The rest of the auditorium was dark. He then told a story that I will never forget.

"You know," he said, "my dad was the one who introduced me to horses." He told how his father was a rancher who ran a big horse stable, well known for its ability to train wild horses. He would watch his father and the men working for him spend many hours with a single horse until, finally—tired and broken—the horse gave up. The spirit was gone and the horse obeyed.

"You see," said Monty, "my father wasn't a horse whisperer, he was a horse breaker!"

For years, Monty had been taught by his father that these wild horses were out of control, with no direction, and that through pain and suffering and being beaten you could eventually get them to summit—to behave, and finally do what they were told. With their spirits gone, the beaten horses would be handed back to their owners, ready to serve and obey. For young Monty, something didn't seem right.

At seventeen, he approached his father with an idea—something quite radical given the environment he was in. But it was an idea Monty was already discovering to be true. He said, "You know Dad, I'm not sure the way you're breaking these horses is the most effective way of getting them to behave compliantly."

"What do you mean?" his dad wondered.

"I think there's a way of approaching these horses that doesn't need the use of whips, sticks, or any kind of force at all. I think there's a way we can train these horses to do what we want them to do by using a more gentle and communicative approach. Through kindness and a better understanding of their behaviour, I think we could get the horses onside in a fraction of the time."

"Don't be ridiculous," his father objected. And with that, the conversation ended.

Monty went on to explain to the crowd how his idea didn't die. His desire to try out his method was unabated. He decided to work privately with his horses, mastering his skill and honing his innate ability to communicate with them.

"Unfortunately, my father died before I was able to show him how it was done," Monty told the audience, as a tear rolled down his cheek. "My greatest regret is that he never got to see how it is done. If he could see me now, I'm sure he would be proud."

"You see," said Monty, "my father raised his children the same way he approached horses. Like a lot of fathers from his time, he would often resort to violence or strong discipline to get us to behave a certain way. Our free spirit and sense of adventure were often misread as being wayward and out of control. Apparently, as the cliché goes, children were meant to be seen and not heard. He had little time for compassion or understanding. He had his way of dealing with things, and that was it."

Monty paused and looked at the crowd: "You see folks, kids are a lot like horses. They are born wild and free. That's their natural way to behave. They were meant to run and explore, to make noises and play. Boys, in particular, weren't meant to sit still and read. Life isn't in a book, it's out there in the fields and forests. It's about risk taking and adventure seeking. Then Monty added, "Your job as a parent isn't to break their wild spirit. It's to communicate with it, to help keep them focused, and do your best to keep them safe. Children don't need to be broken, they need to be held, loved, and guided."

I looked around at the audience and saw many people sitting quietly, nodding their heads in agreement. Some had tears running down their cheeks. Others were possibly contemplating their own lives. Monty's talk was universal—a message to us all about how to treat not only our own children, but *all* children.

As I reflected on my own life with my two boys, I gently smiled to myself. I felt my heart go warm. I thought of the wonderful time I was having being a dad. But mostly I knew that for me…well, I felt was doing okay. My two boys certainly had spirit, and I enjoyed and celebrated that part of them the most. They brought an energy into the house that Jules and I thrived on, and all we had to do was nurture it the best way we could.

When I finally said goodbye to Monty, I did so with a sense of sadness, like watching your grandfather walk off into the sunset. But then, I guess, that's what cowboys do. With the words of an old Willy Nelson song playing in the background, Monty slowly rode out of the auditorium.

Sometimes people come into your life for a reason and change you in ways you never expected. Monty was one of those guys for me and probably hundreds, if not thousands, of others around the world.

16

LOST IN SPACE

In 2003 as I sat listening in a university lecture room in Perth to a talk by Gregg Braden, I heard him warn his audience by saying, "The problem we face as a species is that we're creating technology faster than the wisdom of how to use it." Those words have rung in my ears for many years and I have since discovered that this is clearly apparent when it comes to raising our children.

When I first started to write this book nearly eight years ago, the digital tsunami that is now sweeping the planet hadn't quite taken the stranglehold on childhood that it has today. This was something that I could never have foreseen a decade ago. The advances in technology, although well-meaning, have created a major challenge to parents the world over.

Though I have already touched on the dangers of technology and screen time on our kids, so profound is this grip on our children that I felt the need to address it one more time in this chapter.

I must admit that of all the challenges Jules and I have faced as parents, the influence of digital technology on our boys' lives is by far our greatest. So big is this digital transformation of the landscape that it's almost impossible to see where it begins and ends. It's like being in the middle of thick fog and looking for the edges. We are currently in the middle of this fog, and the challenge I face here is actually writing about something we're dealing with right now.

Many people are probably unaware that family time has dropped by almost a third in the last decade. Jules and I have recently felt that screens were, and still are, slowly taking our boys' attention away from us in the evenings.

In their ground-breaking book *Hold on to your Kids*, Gordon Neufeld Ph.D. and Dr. Gabor Mate M.D. suggest that the biggest threat the digital world plays in the raising of our children is peer orientation. In the introduction to this book, I said that as a father, I wanted to be my boys' "best bet." I suggested that, as parents, we need to make sure that we do all we can to be a major influence in their lives. We are the ones who should make the strongest connection we can and hopefully pass on to them a strong sense of values as well as give them direction in life. Without the distraction of a digital world, this used to be a tried and trusted path for parents to follow. Not anymore.

Research tells us that nearly 80% of children are now accessing screens before the age of two. That's unbelievable! Incredibly, young people between the ages of eight and eighteen now spend an average of over ten hours a day on their screens. Parents everywhere are competing continuously for their children's attention. Like a drug consumed *en masse*, children across the western world are becoming *addicted* to their screens...what has happened?

According to many experts, there are concerns that overuse of screen time has a dangerous effect on the brain development of young kids. Joseph Chilton Pearce, who lectures on this area, suggests that when a child sits in front of a screen streaming information, the higher cortical regions of the brain will immediately recognise that they are no longer required and begin to shut down. Computer screen images, being concrete rather than abstract forms, are like junk food in this respect, empty calories that displace the nutrients needed for growth. Apparently the particular centres of the brain necessary for critical and creative thinking are not engaged while a child is absorbed in screen time. Over time, the parts of the brain that aren't being used in those developing early years of childhood begin to degenerate.

In fact, research suggests there is now a negative correlation between screen time and language acquisition. When children are behind screens, it evokes a tuning out response from the brain. In his book *Magical Child*, Joseph goes on to say that the most important ingredient in a child's brain development is play. Screen time is therefore substituting for children's natural play time and stifling their brain development. The brain doesn't develop through input, but rather by emerging into one's world. Armed with this information, you can realise why I was so keen on building treehouses, or taking the boys to the park to play as often as I could.

While our boys were growing up, Jules and I did our best to keep technology at arm's length. In fact, besides the two TVs in the house, our boys rarely spent much time in front of screens at all. Were we to raise our boys in the current environment, I'm not entirely sure if things would have been that easy. As the boys got older, we continually resisted the need to bring technology into their lives. To this day, I'm certain that we made the right choice in delaying their access to too much technology. In fact, when I look back, I remember clearly that it was the education system that finally forced our hand into bringing "screens" into their lives well before we wanted to. At eleven years of age, Cody progressed on his journey to high school and we were told that in order to participate in the school curriculum all parents were to purchase a laptop for each child…and so the addiction began.

Of course, the powers that be will tell you that these screens now give children access to information that most of us could never have dreamed of. The advantages of being connected to a digital world does mean that our children have access to resources to help them with their studies, even when their teachers aren't around. These advances make it easier for our children to finish assignments outside of the classroom, and ultimately revolutionise the way we educate them.

But is this really what's happening?

The basic flaw in this assumption is that it's information that our children are seeking. Not surprisingly, when it comes to engaging with the digital world, our children are not after scholastic information. Many of our children access the cyber world simply for entertainment; however, even that takes a distant second place in the search for what our children are ultimately seeking. The number one reason children access the digital world is … connection.

The digital devices designed to serve schools and businesses have now been repurposed to connect our peer-oriented children with one another. The digital revolution has become, for all intents and purposes, a phenomenon of social connectivity. Human beings, often as adults, but especially as immature young creatures, are hungry for information, not about the world but about their attachment status.

Apparently the problem isn't so much that screen time "isn't what they need." The problem is that "it *interferes* with what they need."

This need to constantly be connected to each other is why "peer-orientation" is now the biggest threat to parenting. As parents we are slowly losing our ability to be the main voice in our children's lives. It makes sense that all family relationships were meant to be hierarchical by nature. This top down approach meant that the wisdom of age allowed for the filtering of the "right" kind of information to be passed down to children from their parents.

Our moral compass came from above, and the values we handed down to our children were based on a life well lived. The safety of a close and intimate environment, surrounded by unconditional love, allowed for strong relationships to unfold as nature intended. Once the front door was closed, the home environment – free from external influences – allowed this parenting paradigm to play out. The game has now changed dramatically.

Family homes are now invaded in every room by connections to the digital world. The front door may be closed, but the intruders are everywhere. Many parents talk of the constant struggle to get their children's attention. Addicted to screens, our children constantly search for connection. Facebook and other forms of social media act like a crack dealers constantly luring our children to their next hit. The sound of, "Come on kids, dinner's ready" is like a distant echo, with our children still glued to their screens, endlessly typing away, seemingly lost in a never ending black hole of comments, likes and dislikes.

It's not uncommon for me to come home from work only to walk in and see my boys glued to their screens. They've got a phone attached to their left hand, a laptop in their right, while the Xbox is on the big TV. At the same time, they converse with friends in cyberspace through a set of head phones.

"Hi boys, Dad's home!" Oh yes, it's affecting us all. Teenage screen addiction is severely on the rise and has evoked paediatric warnings across the country. According to a University of Southern California survey, 89% of today's parents don't see the amount of time their children spend on the internet as problematic. Unfortunately, in today's society, what is normal is often judged by what it typical, not by what is natural or what is healthy.

The problem with peer-oriented attachment is that it rarely fills the kind of attachment hunger our children need. I previously wrote about the fact that the internet is often a wounding environment, filled with miscommunication and judgment. Without the wisdom of age and a capacity for reverence, "other children" rarely have the ability to take a loving, non-judgmental approach to their peers' concerns. Instead, a lot of the advice that's delivered online isn't really what they need.

As parents, one of our most significant responsibilities is to act as the buffer between our children and society. In order to raise our children properly, we need them to be dependent on us, the way nature intended. There used to be a time when the parents were the holders of the knowledge in the house. If a child needed a question answered, they would eagerly run to Mum or Dad. This is no longer the case. We are being replaced by search engines, which are undermining our ability to control both content and context.

Imagine a little girl looking out the window in the evening and asking, "Daddy, what are stars?" Now a quick search of Google would talk about bursts of gas and hydrogen. Compare that to a loving father's response. "You see, darling, the stars are the eyes of everyone in heaven. The brightest one just there is your Aunt Molly. She watches over you at night time and keeps you safe. She is there if you ever want to talk to her and sends you love through your window as you drift off to sleep every night." The difference is context.

With the digital invasion, our children are no longer looking to us for company. They now have each other. The problem, however, is this constant need to be in touch. What are they searching for? What's the addiction? Gordon Neufeld sums it up beautifully here:

> *"The problem is that the technological attachment activity our children are engaging in acts like a persistent and pervasive weed that eventually takes over the garden, crowding out all other plants that are rooted there. Worryingly, digitally mediated social connections interfere with what children truly need. The whole purpose of attachment is to find release, to be able to rest from the urgent need to find attachment. Growth emanates from this place of rest. If attachment activity doesn't lead to fulfilment, it cannot forward maturation: the anxiety is*

too great, the vulnerability too unbearable. For emotional growth children need to stay vulnerable, and to be able to stay vulnerable, they need to feel secure."

Making sure the boys always felt secure was a priority for Jules and me. They constantly witnessed our close and loving relationship. Rarely were they exposed to shouting or screaming; conversely, our house was a loving place, full of kind words and warm hearts. Knowing that they felt safe and secure allowed us to build a strong, loving connection with them both. Like many children their age, they still spend many hours connected to their peer groups and there are times when we wish they were more present with us. To offset this, we make sure that dinner time is always spent with the screens off. We chat openly about their day and discuss any problems they might be having. We don't feel overly threatened by their peer group attachments. That's not to say we are always happy with them, but we are also smart enough to know that we can't fight this need for our boys to have this digital connection.

Instead, we spend a lot of time getting to know who their friends are. We have very close relationships not only with their friends, but with the parents as well. We consciously set out to get to know who their school friends were from very early on, most of them from kindergarten. In a way, a lot of these boys are family to us and feel very comfortable in our house. When they were young, they often had sleepovers. Using our bathroom to brush their teeth, changing into their pyjamas, and then jumping into their sleeping bags in our living room meant we acted as surrogate parents while they were in our care. Birthday parties and school functions allowed us to get to know all the parents, many of whom are now our closest friends.

This kind of real-world, face-to-face contact means that most of the kids they talk to online understand the emotional gaps that a digital world doesn't allow for. They rarely experience cyber bullying because of these real-world attachments. I'm not suggesting it doesn't happen, or won't in the future, but kids whose attachment needs are met are less likely to be drawn into the type of cyber bullying that we see so prominently today.

The key to overcoming the pitfalls of our peer-oriented children lies solely in our *relationship* with them. If we become absent fathers or distant mothers, our children are vulnerable. If the house they live in doesn't feel safe and secure, our children are vulnerable. If we don't make the time to get to know their circle of friends, once again – they are vulnerable. It is our job as parents to make sure that we make them feel safe and secure in their vulnerability in order for them to grow and learn. Our children long for a deep connection; if they don't get it at home, they will search for it online.

Never before have we been more exposed as parents. The society we have all created now demands that both parents join the work force. Across the country, many children are coming home to vacant houses. Longing for some sort of connection, they immediately turn to their peers online. Here they begin to create their own families and find, if not a deep connection, at least a form of attachment that breaks the loneliness of an empty house. After a while, this connection starts to become more familiar than the one at home.

We must guide our children and refuse to leave them hungry for attachment. Spending quality time with them as often as possible fulfils their attachment needs. Rituals and routines that they can depend on and look forward to are the key. Soccer training twice a week with Dad. Dinner time with the family. Weekends with grandparents. Saturday morning shopping, coffee, and cake with Mum. Bedtime stories in the evenings. These are all opportunities to alleviate that need for our children to find attachment online. It will inoculate them from the attachment addictions that are plaguing many of their friends.

If our relationships with our children are strong, respectful, and serve their needs, then they will go online for entertainment more than anything else. The deeper we can cultivate the vital relationship with our children, the more they can hold on to us even when we are not around physically. Although for many parents, screen time can still be an annoying distraction, there's comfort in the fact that they know they still hold the strongest place in their children's hearts. That loving attachment will outshine anything their kids will ever find in the digital world.

17

THE SCIENCE OF COMPASSION

In July of 2005, I was sitting in the Kathmandu airport when, out of the corner of my eye, I noticed Gregg Braden. I watched as he stood up and started to walk toward me. I remember thinking at the time there wasn't anyone else in the world that I would rather journey into the mountains of Tibet with than Gregg.

I first saw Gregg Braden give a talk at the University of Western Australia in November, 2003. As I sat in the UWA lecture theatre listening to his talk, I remember thinking that I had never before heard someone talk so beautifully and eloquently, and with so much passion, about things that were so important. Gregg was known around the world as one of the most progressive thinkers on the planet, and the author of many wonderfully thought-provoking books, such as *Awakening to Zero Point*, *The Isaiah Effect*, *Walking between the Worlds*, and *The God Code.*" Gregg is also one of the world's leading experts on "The Dead Sea Scrolls."

He had worked as a geologist for Philips petroleum before moving to CISCO systems as a computer software designer. Then he worked for NASA in their weapons design area. However, after many years in the hard sciences, he gave it all away and spent the next eighteen years studying most of the main religions of the world. He became an expert on the Christian traditions, the ancient Essenes and the Tibetan culture.

Gregg's thirst for the deeper meaning of life drew me to him and his work. I think at some point in our lives we all begin to ask ourselves the Big Four questions:

Who I am?

Where did I come from?

Why am I here?

Where am I going?

These perennial philosophical questions nurture the soul, and have the ability to breathe life into an otherwise dull existence. They allow for, and even invite, moments of clarity and equilibrium in a sea of confusion. For many, however, if and when these fleeting moments occur, they are viewed as self-indulgent interruptions to the "real issues" of a busy life. Tackling the big questions demands a lot of focus and attention, yet rarely leads to conclusive answers. Without the immediate relief of an instant answer, we impatiently get on with whatever else we were "meant to be doing."

But not Gregg. I'm not sure which attracted me most: the opportunity to spend sixteen days with this great man or the alluring name of the expedition—"In Search of Original

Wisdom and the Science of Compassion." Either way, I willingly paid good money to join the group. Once again with Jules's blessing, I left her behind to look after our two beautiful little boys as I embraced yet another part of my journey into fatherhood.

Back at the crowded airport in Kathmandu, Gregg had made a beeline straight for me, hand outstretched.

"I believe you're one of the two Australians on the expedition?" he asked. I shook his hand, and immediately felt at ease as he gave me a warm welcoming smile.

Gregg sat down next to me and began to ask about my life.

"Are you married?" he asked.

"Yes I am … ten years in June," I replied.

He turned and looked me straight in the eye, "Darrell, tell me, what's the secret to a successful marriage?"

I stared back at him, thinking this was some sort of rhetorical question. I paused, waiting for him to finish. After all, here was a guy who lectures across the globe about the mysteries of the world, a *New York Times* best-selling author who has written books about God, compassion, consciousness, and our connection to all things. Was he really asking me, a guy he has known for five minutes, for marital advice?

Actually, he was. I didn't know at the time that Gregg had recently tied the knot for the first time.

The pause seemed to go on forever until I realised that he was waiting for my response. Unprepared, I simply went to my heart and spoke as honestly as I could.

"You know Gregg, I think if you look at any successful relationship, you will find that the ones that grow strong and stand the test of time are those where both parties are continually contributing to the relationship. I think the problem with a lot of marriages is that both parties are looking to see what they can 'get' from the marriage. They are looking for the other person to make them happy. They are always asking 'what's in it for me?' 'What am I getting from this?'"

Gregg listened with interest as I continued to offer my perspective.

"When relationships first begin, they usually go well because both parties are keen to be involved. They look for ways to make the other person happy—the courting, flirting stage. When that happens, they both enjoy the experience because both contribute much and, therefore, each receives at the same time. However, as time passes, this often begins to fade, and people begin taking each other for granted and taking from the relationship, expecting more and more from the other person."

I felt like I had said enough, but he remained silent, so I kept going. I was full of the subject and my own passion infused me as I spoke. "When they stop being happy, couples begin to blame each other. If both constantly take from the relationship, soon there's nothing left. Sometimes, only one person gives while the other just takes. Even though these relationships can last a long time, they are rarely a happy experience, especially for the person doing all the giving."

I told Gregg that when I met Jules, I knew her love for me was unconditional. She was always thinking about how she could make my life happier. Although we have challenges and struggles, like every couple, our focus was always about making each other happy. We both contribute to the relationship more than we take. So, of course, our relationship is always growing stronger. That's really what a life of service is all about. All the avatars that ever walked this planet, and extraordinary people like Mother Teresa, Nelson Mandela, Gandhi, knew that the key to finding peace and happiness is encapsulated in the mantra, "How may I serve?" not, "How may I take?" Why should marriage, or any relationship, be any different?

The "secret" is to realise that ultimate happiness will never come from taking, only from giving. That's why couples who have been married for fifty years, who always have a smile on their face and peace in their heart, usually live a simple existence. I'll never forget the opening lines from *The Notebook*, one of the best films I've ever seen about a lasting, loving relationship:

> *I am no one special, just a common man with common thoughts. I've led a common life. There are no monuments to me, and my name will soon be forgotten. But in one respect, I've succeeded as gloriously as anyone who ever lived. For I have loved another with all my heart and soul, and for me, that has always been enough.*

Gregg gave me a knowing smile and a warm embrace, and suggested we talk more during the trip. A voice over the loudspeaker told us that our flight from Kathmandu to Lhasa, the capital of Tibet, was now boarding. As I walked across the tarmac and onto the plane, I thought about how humble it was for Gregg to reach out for answers in his personal life while at the same time he wrote and spoke to the world about the problems we face as a species. Though I admired him before I met him, I now knew that I was with the right person to guide me through this mystical land. Gandhi once said that one the greatest qualities a human being can have is humility. I couldn't agree more.

Our group had met in Kathmandu so we could begin to acclimatize before landing in the high altitudes of Tibet. This mountainous country was still relatively untouched by the Western world but, as we soon find out, all that was about to change.

Gregg explained to us that the Tibetans were great record keepers and that, hidden in the temples and monasteries of this ancient land, were the records of nearly every religion on Earth. Tibetans have always been nomadic and travelled many miles across many continents collecting and recording ancient texts and scriptures from all religions. As we visited the temples and sat with the monks and nuns, we realised these were the current-day guardians of a huge body of knowledge, so precious to our modern world. Gregg remarked that you can go to the temples of Egypt and look at the hieroglyphics on the walls, but the men who wrote those are long gone. Yet here in Tibet, we encountered a living, breathing culture that still embodied the ancient wisdom of one of the world's greatest spiritual cultures.

We soon found out that Gregg was deeply trusted by the people of this land and welcomed by the Tibetan dignitaries. Through his connections, we gained access to monasteries and temples that most Western tourists would never be allowed to see. In fact, on one occasion we were secretly escorted into a sacred room that not even local Tibetans had access to. As we entered the room, a local pilgrim took the opportunity and pretended to be part of our group. The temple guardians quickly grabbed her and ushered her out. I realised how fortunate we were to be travelling with Gregg Braden, and felt a deep sense of gratitude for being allowed to enter such sacred places.

While our relationship with the Tibetans was consistently positive, being with Gregg meant the Chinese military watched us closely and carefully. Before we even arrived, we were warned that tourists sympathetic to the Tibetan cause were not welcome, and that we had to be prepared to be searched at stops along the way. Gregg reminded us of the most alarming piece of information of all.

The Tibetan people love and adore their beloved leader, the Dalai Lama. They prayed to His Holiness every day, and read from his teachings. However, to the Chinese military, he is seen as a separatist and traitor for advocating Tibetan self-rule. When the Chinese invaded, he fled from Tibet in 1959, and now leads a government from exile in India. Under Chinese military rule, the Tibetans know that if they are ever caught with a picture of the Dalai Lama, they would be sent to a Chinese prison and probably never be seen again. As visitors to Tibet, we were told the same rules now applied to us. Gregg warned us that their threats were serious, and that under no circumstances should we carry his picture with us.

Over the ensuing days and weeks, we met many of the local people. Because of Gregg's connections, we were invited into their monasteries, temples, and homes. We travelled through mountain ranges layered among a sea of yellow flowers. As we gradually climbed into the more remote parts of the country, we noticed that many roads had almost been washed away, making our journey more treacherous by the mile. I remember looking down as the bus's wheels came dangerously close to the edges of the road. One slip and we would surely plummet down into the ravine. We were told that the Chinese military made sure the roads weren't fixed because they didn't want to encourage tourists to visit the monasteries. As a result, our determination to visit these people and tell the world about their plight grew even stronger.

On arriving at ancient temples, we were invited to chant with the monks. We drank warm yak milk and sang songs with the nuns. They told us stories of how the Chinese had taken their sons and daughters and destroyed their temples. But they also spoke of forgiveness and compassion and, of course, they always spoke of their love for the Dalai Lama. Once, after singing with the nuns, we were invited individually to visit where they lived. They all had their own small room, protected by steel gates heavily locked from the inside.

To my amazement, I saw pictures of the Dalai Lama pinned to the walls of their rooms. Their love for His Holiness outweighed the risk. The locked steel gates provided their only protection against the snooping Chinese military. If the pictures were discovered, the Chinese would surely have dragged off the nuns, most likely never to be seen again. Yet, in the face of such persecution, the Tibetan people remained, calm, loving, compassionate, and peaceful.

We travelled through country by bus with our own private driver. Gregg used this time to talk to us about the challenges faced by the Tibetans. In the temples and on the streets, the Chinese watched us closely, so if Gregg wanted to tell us anything even slightly contentious he would say, "… and I will save the rest of that story for the bus!" The bus became our sanctuary for private conversations. We were told not to record any of it, as we could be pulled over at any time and asked to hand over our cameras or voice recorders for inspection. As a result, while I was with the nuns, I was careful not to take any pictures with the Dalai Lama in the background. As much as I wanted to, I knew that if the Chinese found the pictures on my camera, the nuns would have been in grave danger.

After visiting the nuns, the next day we drove into the centre of town. On the way, Gregg explained that we were going to visit a classroom where a group of young monks was being taught by a high lama. We filed off the bus one at a time and were led down an alleyway into a small temple. The students sat on the ground with their textbooks open, listening astutely to their master teacher. We were directed to walk around the teacher to the other side of the room. As we moved among the students, I was struck by the beautiful welcoming smiles on every single face. Even the teacher took time to look up and offer a warm smile to each one of us.

At no time did I get a sense that our presence interfered with their daily lives. They were so happy we had taken the time to visit them. They sat calmly listening to their teacher while greeting us with love and a natural curiosity. Their warmth was contagious, and we all returned their friendly smiles. They were happy to welcome visitors who respected their culture and expressed interest in learning about it.

Later that night, I reflected on the experience. How could a simple walk through a classroom affect me so deeply? Gregg wanted us to experience the beauty, courage, and nobility of Tibetan culture—not just to read about it, but to directly *experience* it firsthand. An entire culture persecuted for more than half a century by a major global power, forbidding the people to even possess a picture of their spiritual leader. Given the atrocities perpetrated on them, they had every reason to be angry. Yet the Tibetans we met showed nothing but love, compassion, and understanding—even for their persecutors. The more I saw of Tibet, the more I loved its people.

Before leaving Australia for Tibet, I had asked my boys if they would be willing to give me some of their precious toy dinosaurs to take with me. We had been told that during our expedition, we would visit an orphanage and were invited to bring any small toys for the children there. As we drove along the broken streets, Gregg explained to us that the children knew we were coming and were excited at the prospect of meeting us. He then put out a proposal: for about $100 US dollars, we could buy all the children new school uniforms, something they would never be able to afford themselves. He asked if we might be willing to try to come up with the money. He needn't have asked twice. Within 20 minutes, before arriving at the orphanage, $720 US dollars had been offered up. We would hand over the money along with ten boxes of fresh fruit, vegetables, and other essentials.

As we entered the gates of the orphanage, we were greeted by thirty to forty children. Though scattily dressed, their fresh faces expressed great joy to see us. We enjoyed a guided tour of the orphanage, visiting their makeshift classrooms, meal areas, and simple sleeping quarters. We were invited to join them for a celebratory meal, during which the children sang traditional Tibetan songs and danced with happiness for this rare chance to meet Westerners. In turn, we responded with songs from our own countries. Although our singing was rough, the children didn't mind at all, often bursting into laughter as we made funny faces and tried our best to entertain them in return.

We then sat in smaller groups and tried our best to communicate. I sat with five young boys, all about the same age as the two I had left behind. Looking into their eyes reminded me of how lucky I was to be a father myself. I felt for these children, as I couldn't think of anything worse than being abandoned by your parents. I did my best not to show my tears, and instead reached into my pocket and brought out a bag full of toy dinosaurs. As I passed a dinosaur to each child, their smiles melted my heart. I explained that the toys were a gift from my boys, and as they held them up I took a photo of this special moment to take back to Cody and Taylor.

We left the orphanage with mixed emotions. Often with such experiences, you feel deep joy and happiness knowing you were able to contribute in a positive way. At the same time, however, I felt an overwhelming sadness knowing that their plight would continue after our departure. I was left with a sense of "maybe I could have done more."

Two weeks later, when we returned to the capital city of Lhasa, Gregg asked us if we were up to visiting the orphanage one more time. This meant dropping other things from our schedule. His suggestion was met with an overriding, *"Yes, please!"* As we approached the gates of the orphanage, we were told to wait on the bus as they had a surprise for us. Most of our group were middle-aged women, many of whom had children of their own, women who had come to Tibet to find meaning and purpose in their own lives.

As the gates of the orphanage opened, that meaning suddenly came racing toward them. With the money we had donated, not only had they been able to purchase uniforms for every child, but also new shoes, school bags, hats, and equipment. They even took all the children to the markets, bought them ice creams and trinkets—a day's outing they could never have imagined.

As we stepped off the bus, we were greeted individually with hugs and tears of joy. I stood watching the women greet the children as if they were their own. We were met by a sea of bright red school uniforms, immaculately dressed children with schools bags in hand, offering welcoming hugs for these once-strangers who now seemed like long-lost relatives. Then a group of young boys ran up to me with dinosaurs in their hands, jumping into my arms as if I was the father they never had. They crashed into me just like Cody and Taylor used to when coming home from school.

For those ready to receive it, the love of small children is universal. They crave closeness and connection, the warmth of a hug and a tender embrace. If just for that moment, their life is good, all their problems and worries pushed aside. It's what every child needs; that is why they didn't want to let us go. And in that moment, neither did I.

I guess we all came to this mystical place looking for our own meaning, trying to make sense of our own lives. For some, returning to their own homes meant many changes. Perhaps a time to forgive those who had betrayed them in the past. Others had a sense of gratitude for the things they left behind. For me, the moment I landed back in Perth, it all made sense. Two little boys ran up to me as fast as their legs could carry them, screaming at the top of their voices, "Daddy's home. Daddy's home!" My beautiful wife stood just behind them, smiling, radiating love.

Yes, it all made sense.

18

THE SECRET TO LIFE

My journey to be a father often meant discovering lessons about life itself. I wanted to have a bigger overarching story for my boys about how important it was to live with passion. In my twenties and thirties I started reading as many books as I could get my hands on. I got caught up in the whole New Age movement and loved stories that spoke to the mystery of life and our universe.

One book in particular stood out for me: Dan Millman's *The Way of the Peaceful Warrior* – a half-fact, half-fiction account of Millman's life. As a young, enthusiastic, and budding Olympic gymnast, he became disillusioned with his life and started searching for his own meaning and life-purpose. A chance meeting with a wise, old mystical shaman (known as "Socrates") changed his life. To casual observers, Socrates spent his time working as a humble gas station attendant. But when he encountered the young gymnast struggling with an existential crisis, Socrates took on the young man as his apprentice. As the shaman guided Millman on his life-changing journey, the frustrated gymnast began to discover a deeper meaning to life.

Toward the end of the book, after many months sharing his wisdom and facilitating life's lessons, Socrates turns to Dan and says, "It's now time for your final lesson Dan… I want you to sit and meditate under the sacred Bodhi tree and only return when you can tell me what the secret to life is."

I couldn't wait to discover the answer. But as I got up to this part in the book, I suddenly realised my plane was about to touch down, my tray table had to be returned to its upright position, and my seat belt had to be fastened. As I looked out the window, I saw the sparse African plains go hurtling by. My thoughts turned to the job at hand, a filming assignment in Tanzania where I was to spend the next couple of weeks. The assignment combined the beauty of an African sunset with the life-threatening encounters of a politically unstable landscape.

We touched down in Dar es Salaam on the East coast of Africa, one of the largest and richest cities in Tanzania. As far as African countries go, this was certainly more friendly than most. I was travelling with Don, a director and close friend, and we were met by the local expat and representative of a research drilling company who had hired us for the shoot.

After meeting at the local office, we headed off to a smaller airport and boarded a six-seater light aircraft that flew us into one of the remotest parts of the country. On arrival, the entire village of curious onlookers came out to greet these fair-skinned travellers. As I got my gear out of the back of the plane, I turned to find myself surrounded by a sea of smiling black faces with glowing white teeth. I stood under the wing of the plane with hundreds of my newfound friends as Don recorded the moment on camera—a photograph that still holds a place in my office today.

We drove on to a small village, and as we arrived, I looked out the window of our old Toyota four wheel drive to see three colourfully dressed African women walking toward an old empty oil drum, carrying three live chickens hanging upturned in their hands. When we got closer, the driver turned and yelled, "That's your lunch!" To my horror, the women slit the chickens' throats, and I watched as the life slowly drained from their bodies. I quickly realised that the world of fast-food and computers was a long way away. We grabbed our camera gear, and were told that the next part of the journey would be on foot. Walking past the three women, I noticed that one had begun to fill the half-open drum with wood for the fire. The other two were busy ripping feathers off the now lifeless chickens. I was mesmerized by their simple existence: wake up, find food, make your meal and eat. Life was about survival; pretty uncomplicated, really.

As we arrived at what seemed to be an abandoned alluvial site full of old diggings and deep holes, our escort informed us that many years ago, rich deposits of gold had been discovered in this area. The lease and tenement agreements were currently held by the multinational corporation that had hired us. I began filming the landscape around me when Don yelled out from about 100 meters away, beckoning me to come over with my camera. I arrived to see two local tribesmen sitting either side of a very, very deep hole. I was told it was an old abandoned mineshaft and that large nuggets of gold could still be found there if you were prepared to dig up the earth at the very bottom. A makeshift winch and a rope, placed across the top of the hole, dropped down into the shaft below. It wasn't anymore than a meter wide, and Don said to keep filming as they slowly wound up the winch.

After what seemed like an eternity, to my astonishment I finally saw the top of a man's head as he began to appear out of the black hole. He arrived covered in mud, only the whites of his eyes showing. He held nothing but a pick and small bucket filled with dirt that he used as a seat as they pulled him up out of the hole. God only knows how long he had been down there without any water. However, this time—like many times before—he had come up without a nugget, but with hope that once he sieved and washed through the bucket of dirt, he might find a few tiny flakes of gold—something he could exchange for money or food. It felt like going back in time. I began to wonder what the meaning of life was to these people.

Over the coming days, we travelled further north and found ourselves near a town called Mwanza, on the shores of Lake Victoria. The locals told us that a few months ago a ferry had arrived packed with villagers. As it came in to berth, many of the passengers ran to one side, hoping to get off first. The old and overcrowded ferry lurched heavily to one side and completely flipped over. Although trapped inside, many were still alive because of the air pocket in the hull. However, the inexperienced rescuers thought they would do the right thing and cut a hole in the top to free those trapped inside. By doing so, they sunk the ferry and hundreds more needlessly died.

We overnighted in a hotel on the edge of the lake and headed off to another drill site in the morning. An experienced guide came with us and warned us to make sure we got back before dark. Bandits and rebel groups prowled the roads between our hotel and our destination. He said they would just as soon as cut our arms off as steal from us. Also, gaping potholes the size of swimming pools dotted the roads, making progress slow, difficult, and dangerous—particularly after dark.

After three hours bumping along the lonely track, we arrived at our destination and completed our filming assignment. I stopped to look around, taking in the moment. Here I was, in the middle of Africa; although it had its dangers, I still found it a beautiful place. I wondered what my friends were doing back in the suburbs of Perth. I looked out across the valley and saw village after village stretching into the distance. The late sun cast an orange glow on the fields as I captured the images with my camera.

It then dawned on me how much time had passed; the evening was already setting in and we still had a long drive back to the safety of our hotel. The driver quickly got us back into the vehicle and put his foot down to make a speedy return. Up ahead, a small river blocked our path, and could be crossed only by car ferry. When we arrived at the crossing, we had to get in line behind a long row of waiting traffic. As we waited, we saw the ferry gates close and were told we'd have to wait forty-five minutes for the next ferry. This meant that our last hour of travel into town would be in the dark.

The concerned look on our driver's face told us this wasn't good. For most of the trip, I had sat in the back of our dual-cab Toyota shaded by a canvas-covered top. I had spent most of the journey there and back riding in the rear with all the camera gear. I enjoyed riding in the back along with all the camera gear. Although the ride was bumpy, I was able to take in the different smells and sights of this rich land, and hear the sounds of the jungle. It felt alive and I didn't want to miss any of it. However, once across the river, the driver stopped and insisted that it was safer for me to sit up front in the cabin. I took his advice seriously and joined the others inside.

After a long day, the bumpy road began to slowly rock me to sleep. It had become my friend. Like an old sailor with sea legs, I had grown fond of the constant rocking of the vehicle. Just as I thought the day was coming to an end, the driver slammed on his brakes and started yelling in Swahili. I saw him grab a gun out of the glove box and get out of the driver's door. I knew this couldn't be good. Don and I instinctively jumped out of the car. As I turned to see what was going on, I saw about a dozen dark-skinned men with machetes in their hands run off into the bush. The driver screamed at us to get back in the vehicle, and hightailed it as fast as he could back to the hotel. My heart pounded as I tried to comprehend what had just happened. When we arrived at the hotel, it all became apparent.

A gang of thieves had been waiting in the thick vegetation at the side of the road. When they spotted a car full of Westerners, they ran out behind our vehicle and one jumped onto the back. They had purposely picked a spot where the potholes were large and where they knew the vehicles would slow down to almost walking pace. Once on the vehicle, one of them hacked a machete through the canvass back and was about to start throwing our cases out to those following behind. Although they were simply after money and valuables, we were told they wouldn't have hesitated to take the life of anyone who got in their way.

The driver had seen the guy jump up onto the back of the truck. When he slammed the brakes suddenly, the guy fell off.

When the bandits saw his gun they all backed away. When they saw Don and me jump out of the car, they probably assumed we had guns as well. What might have seemed like a gutsy move was mostly just our stupidity. About a dozen bandits had disappeared into the bushes, so we would have been clearly outnumbered. That's when I saw something that made my heart skip a beat. Just thirty minutes earlier, I had been sitting right where the machete had sliced through the canvas! The driver smiled at me and said, "You are a lucky man...that could have been your head." He was the only one smiling.

After a sleepless night, I rose early the next morning thinking about how lucky I had been. It's funny how the smallest of choices can make such a big difference to our lives. Our life-paths can change drastically in a single heartbeat. Perhaps the secret to life lies somewhere in these ponderings?

We packed up the car and began our return trip to Dar es Salaam. Once there, we drove another three hours to Iringa. The paved road gave us a sense of safety in contrast to the one we had left behind. We headed to a protected wildlife park—our final destination and a place I had wanted to see my whole life.

As we travelled along the road, my thoughts turned to my older brother. About twenty years earlier, he had left the safety of the suburbs of Perth to teach at a school in Iringa. When he arrived at the school, it had no running water or electricity. I admired him for the courage it must have taken to come here. At the same time, I envied his experience. How strange that so many years later, here I was travelling down a road he must have seen plenty of times. We passed a sign telling us we had just entered a wildlife park. No gates, no fences...just a sign. I watched as giraffes walked past only meters from our vehicle—

strange to see them without some sort of protective boundary between us. Seeing them so free and accessible fascinated me. Further on, we passed a broken-down truck. Two men changed the tyre while another sat on the roof of the truck, eyes fixed on the horizon.

"He's watching out for a lion!" our driver yelled. Apparently, many villagers had been taken by lions when they had stopped to fix their cars. I kept reminding myself…no fences! *There are no fences!*

That night, we made camp around an open fire. Two men stood guard with guns while the rest of us ate and listened to stories about this great land. The sounds of elephants, lions, and a menagerie of wildlife formed the background to this amazing landscape. When the fire settled and we turned in for the night, I looked up to see the most amazing sky I have ever witnessed. Staring up at a galaxy of stars shining brighter than I had ever seen before, sparkling in a rich, deep-blue sky, put human life in perspective—all very humbling. Of all the planets in the universe, I was fortunate enough to pick this one.

When we finally returned to Dar es Sallam, we decided to take a quick boat trip to the island of Zanzibar. We couldn't have picked a better way to spend our last day in Africa. Zanzibar is well known for its spices, which were a big part of the trade through the area. The crystal-clear turquoise water and pristine white beaches looked like something I had only seen on someone's screensaver. I bathed in the water and swam with the local wildlife before returning to our hotel in the evening.

The next morning as I boarded the plane, I could hardly wait to return to my book, *The Way of the Peaceful Warrior*. Thirty-five thousand feet up, I still searched for the secret to life. As I turned the page and began to read, a warm glow slowly came over me—a deep knowing of truth.

Dan finally returns from the Bodhi tree where he had been meditating for the past two weeks and kneels in front of Socrates, his shaman-mentor. He raises his head and says, "No ordinary moments." A glint sparkles in the old man's eyes.

"That's right Dan…in life, every second is precious."

There are no ordinary moments.

I looked out the window and watched as the sun set over the African plains. I smiled quietly to myself, grateful for my life—perhaps not so much for the adventures, but more for the understanding of how precious every moment is. If there's one message I try to communicate to the boys, it's that each morning you wake up you get to have another go at this thing called life. Don't waste a day boys….in fact don't waste a moment.

19

THE MYSTIC, THE ELDER, AND THE ROCK

I reached over and lifted the blind on my small oval window. The bright light shattered the darkness, reflecting off my tray table and woke the lady next to me who was probably trying her best to get some sleep. The sparse but vibrant red earth below and the vast brilliant blue sky above made a striking contrast. It also reminded me I was getting closer to central Australia. We flew low over the scorched outback—a hot and unforgiving place inhabited by native animals, a proud indigenous culture, a big red rock, and a bucket-load of tourists.

A month earlier, I had received a phone call from Jeremy, a good friend who was now a client of mine. He asked if I would be interested in shooting a spiritual documentary with a wise Aboriginal elder by the name of Bob Randall. Jeremy ran a company called "Transformational Tours," which flew groups to sacred sites around the world. His tours were often guided by scholars and celebrated authors well versed on the origins of each particular expedition destination. I had met Jeremy many years ago while studying NLP and our friendship had blossomed over time. In fact, he and I were roommates on my trip to Tibet with Gregg Braden, an experience that bonded us forever.

Jeremy was now living near Byron Bay on the southeast coast of Australia, and it was great to see that wonderful bald head and big smiling face as he waited to greet me and my assistant, Anthony, at the Uluru airport in the middle of Australia's outback. Jeremy had a car waiting to pick us up, along with our five cases of camera equipment.

Someone else was there to greet me, too: Andrew Harvey, a renowned spiritual teacher, mystic, and author, who would soon become not only a dear and close friend but also a strong voice on the next part of my life's journey. I had briefly met him previously in Sydney, and he joined us on this cinematic expedition.

I was delighted to have this celebrated author as the host of our documentary. The son of an Indian police commissioner, and educated at Oxford, Andrew Harvey had written many books, including the highly acclaimed *The Hope: A Guide to Sacred Activism*. Andrew and Jeremy had worked together taking groups to sacred sites in various parts of Europe and Africa, and had formed a close friendship. Andrew was also a world-renowned expert on the writings of the Sufi poet Rumi, someone I had often quoted at my events in Perth. Now they had teamed up to shoot a documentary about Bob Randall and his relationship with Uluru (formerly known as Ayers Rock), one of the most sacred places on Earth. I felt privileged to join them as the cinematographer.

I took an instant liking to Andrew because of his warm smile and humble persona. A distinguished-looking man, Andrew sported swept-back, shoulder-length hair, and often wore a red cravat that suggested an out-of-work actor. Andrew and Jeremy greeted me with warm, welcoming hugs. Like long-lost friends, we spoke the whole way from the airport to Bob Randall's humble desert residence, catching up on each other's lives.

Soon, however, our chatter turned to silence. As I looked out the window of our four-wheel drive, it suddenly dawned on me why we, like so many before us, had made the great trek to this most sacred place. I pushed my head out the window and immediately felt the warm air rush against my face. I tried to get a better look at this remarkable site—which would form the backdrop to our spiritual adventure over the next few days: rising out of the earth in all its breath-taking glory—*Uluru!*

This three-hundred-million-year-old massive monolith in Australia's Red Centre majestically stands out as the spiritual heart of the great southern land. A geological wonder and cultural marvel, the great red rock towers up from the desert, dominating the surrounding terrain. Uluru remains a sacred place to the Anangu people who have lived in the region for thousands of years, and whose spiritual beliefs charge them with the responsibility of looking after the land. Thirty-five kilometres to the west stands the thirty-six rock domes of Kata Tjuta, also a profoundly spiritual location, full of vibrational power and natural beauty. The desert landscape itself teems with unexpected wildlife, splashes of vibrant colour, and, as I was soon to discover, an amazing transformational energy.

As we pulled into Bob's ramshackle place, I saw how close he lived to Uluru itself. The ancient red rock loomed over us like a guardian. As a listed traditional caretaker of Uluru, Bob was one of the few privileged people on Earth allowed to live in the shadows of this sacred site. We were so close, in fact, I felt I could pick up a rock and almost hurl it to the base of this majestic mountain. Being invited to stay at the heart of this spectacular site felt both humbling and a great privilege.

Our boots immediately left footprints in the dusty red dirt when we stepped out of the truck. We grabbed our gear and headed toward the house. Bob Randall, an honoured Aboriginal elder who embodied the wisdom of an entire culture, greeted us. Like so many of his kind, Bob was a victim of "the stolen generation"—countless Aboriginal children taken from their families by the Australian government in the 1940s, and either sent to institutions or adopted out. At age seven, the pain of separation from his natural parents, along with the subsequent hardships he must have endured, would have left most people filled with anger and hatred for white Australians. But not Bob.

I reached out my hand as he welcomed me to his land. As I looked into his eyes, I couldn't help but be reminded of the gentle, forgiving smiles that constantly beamed at me from the people of Tibet.

"You blokes must be thirsty! Come inside and let's get you a drink," Bob announced.

Having lost his first wife, Bob shared his house with Barbara, a wonderful, warm-hearted American woman from Manhattan who had instantly fallen head-over-heels in love with both Bob and the landscape that surrounded him. Having visitors drop by to stay a few nights was not an uncommon experience for them, and the two old caravans parked in his backyard were a sure sign we weren't the first privileged guests to be welcomed into their home. Anthony and I climbed into one of the caravans and threw our personal bags on the beds. Through a small rear window, we had a clear view of Uluru that seemed to be constantly changing colour with the time of day.

Bob lit the barbeque grill for our evening meal while we all sat outside enjoying cold drinks and planning our filming schedule for the next few days. We decided we would shoot the master interview between Andrew and Bob on the morning of the first full day. On day two, we would walk with Bob around the base of Uluru while he told us the story of the Rainbow Serpent. Finally, on day three we would journey across to Kata Tjuta to shoot some overlay of this other awe-inspiring monument. We would travel home on the fourth day.

We spent the rest of the evening sitting under the stars while Bob played the guitar and sang many songs about his people and the land, songs he is now famous for. I sat silently as the wise elder shared stories of his life. A man dedicated to teaching and sharing Aboriginal culture, he spoke eloquently about his vision for reconciliation between Aboriginals and the white man.

He told us that his father was one of the many white men who were given grants over this land to run cattle and sheep stations. In those days, it was quite common for tribal Aboriginal women to have babies from the white men who settled in the outback.

The son of a mixed-race marriage, Bob enjoyed a wholesome childhood growing up on a cattle station while retaining his heritage, constantly surrounded by his native aunts and uncles.

"Some of my most vivid childhood memories are of times when we'd come across certain vegetation, and one of the mothers would tell us a story about the plant. The mothers would draw stories on the ground with their fingers or sticks. We were continually given information about our environment through the creation stories of *Tjukurrpa*. This is how we grew up with the knowledge that everything in nature was part of our family," he said.

More than once during the evening's conversation, Bob pointed out how spirituality is the ultimate answer to reconciliation in this country. He wove Aboriginal spirituality throughout his stories like a rainbow serpent.

I looked up at the night sky sparkling with a trillion stars, and it reminded me of the African skies I had slept under in Tanzania. I thought about how fortunate I had been to travel to such amazing places and to meet so many exceptional people like Bob. I thought about the day when, as a sixteen-year-old, I was told there weren't any jobs as a cameraman. I thought about the book I was reading at the time in Africa and about Dan Millman's discovery about the secret to life: "No ordinary moments."

How right that teaching was. In life, there are no ordinary moments…every breath we take is precious. Too often we forget that gift of life.

I stared at the magical night sky above me and felt the universe staring back. I looked over to Uluru that, once again, had changed colour. Backlit by the full-moon, the entire scene shimmered with a light blue hue that framed the top edge of the rock.

I knew for certain this was no ordinary moment.

The next morning, we found an ideal location for Andrew to conduct the interview. I framed Bob's face in the camera and made sure we could see the morning sunlight gently kissing

Uluru over his right shoulder. He wore his usual cowboy hat, and I managed to bounce some fill-light into the shadow on his face. Out of shot, Andrew took his place alongside me and the camera. I looked forward with excitement, intrigued to see where Andrew would take this conversation.

Andrew Harvey was a celebrated interviewer. Having worked with the BBC, he brought with him a great deal of professionalism. However, what impressed me more than his knowledge was his passion for the subject matter, a passion that even rivalled Bob's.

Andrew is known as an important teacher for his work on "sacred activism." In *The Hope*, he asks all of us to stand up and take responsibility for our planet. To see the sacred in the ordinary, and to understand that true joy can be realised only when we offer our heart and hand in service to each other.

Here I was with two great warriors of our time, sitting at the feet of a unique and sacred site. I hit the record button on my camera, looked over at Andrew, and gave him the nod.

"Bob, tell me the story of *kanyini*"," Andrew opened.

Kanyini drew both Andrew to Bob and this land and it bonded the two of them. Bob explained how *kanyini* is the principle of connectedness through caring and responsibility that underpins Aboriginal life.

"Throughout my life, old men would point to a forest of trees, or a grove, and refer to it as 'people.' See that mob over there? This way of talking could refer to kangaroos, trees, hills, or humans. I discovered that the idea of connecting with all things was quite common through the different Aboriginal nations."

He continues, "All this comes from *tjukurrpa*. This is the bigger consciousness of something that was, and is, the way to live in harmony with all things." The warm smile on Andrew's face said it all.

"Go on, Bob" Andrew encouraged.

"Living this is a matter of how we do things in the present. So when we think about time, it is only the now, the present that is important. In each and every moment of 'now-ness' —that's where we live out the truth of the connectedness of *kanyini*."

My mind flashed back to my bush walks with our young boys through the property at the Margaret River house. Bob's words gave me comfort that connecting them to nature at a young age was time well spent. Little did I realise that I, too, was passing on the great Aboriginal teachings of *kanyini*.

Later that night, we again sat outside under the stars and spoke about life. Surrounded by a group of people I admired greatly and trusted completely, the conversation eventually turned to my background. Andrew, in particular, expressed a keen interest in my upbringing and my thoughts about raising boys. We spoke about the "sacred feminine" in men, a subject that interested Andrew greatly. How do men balance their masculine and feminine aspects? How do we open up emotionally to each other? These questions soon became the focus of the evening's discussion. I told Andrew about my desire to raise my boys with a healthy amount of receptive *yin* and active *yang*. I spoke about the warrior inside my two boys, and about their need to express themselves emotionally in other ways.

Andrew and Bob both shared words of wisdom and at the same time were obviously moved by the passion in my voice as I spoke about raising my boys into fully grounded young men. When we talk from the deepest parts of our heart, we quickly connect on a deeper level with those around us. The topic of men here in Australia (in fact, in most Western countries) became an important talking point between Andrew and me. So many men seem to find it hard to open up and talk from the heart. It was nice to be in the company of such a well-balanced group—all strong warriors with the courage to open their hearts and speak their own truth, a rare experience in today's world.

Toward the end of the night, the conversation returned to planning the next day's filming. We would follow Bob to some especially sacred parts of the base of Uluru—places the general public is not allowed to enter. Bob would tell the story of the rainbow serpent and its relationship to Uluru. He told us that a long time ago, in the "Dreamtime" before there were men or animals or anything, there was the Rainbow Serpent, or rainbow snake as it is sometimes called, the mother of us all. She moved around in the darkness before the sun and the moon appeared in the sky; she created mountain ranges and deep valleys as her serpentine body slid across the land.

Wherever she thrashed her body, great rifts appeared in the earth, and she left behind big hollows where her body had lain asleep. In time, the moment arrived to create life on Earth, and at the place called Uluru, the great mother Rainbow Serpent gave birth to all of life.

As we sat around the table listening intently to Bob's stories of the magical serpent, a loud yell from Anthony broke the silence.

"What the hell! "I turned to see a huge python slithering out from the darkness under our caravan, heading straight toward us. I had never seen such a huge snake; it stretched about two-and-a-half meters in length.

"Quick," Bob reacted, "we need to grab her before she comes inside." For some strange reason, Bob was looking right at me.

"Who are you talking to, Bob?" I asked.

"You two young blokes...you need to catch her and put her in a bag!" he announced.

In an earlier chapter, I mentioned that my biggest fear in the world was needles. Well, I lied. It's *snakes*!

"Are you serious, Bob?" I shot back, desperately hoping he was joking. "Can't we just close the doors and let her go on her way?"

"No, she's way too big to have living near the property," Bob replied. "She could easily strangle a young child." Bob was right. The snake was massive!

Bob threw me a rake and handed Anthony a hessian bag. Without time to think, I quickly put the rake in front of the snake and watched with fear as the python slowly slid up onto it and toward me. Lifting the rake, I suddenly discovered how truly huge this snake was. I could barely keep the weight of this thing off the ground. To make things worse, the big yellow python had enough strength that although I had lifted it completely off the ground it still managed to keep itself upright, continuing to slide up the handle of the rake, inching its way toward me. I could clearly see its tongue flicking in and out, now only a few feet from my face.

"Quick," I yelled to Anthony, "grab its tail and throw it in the bag."

"I'm not bloody touching it!" he shot back. "I've got the bag open, you drop it in!" Like a scene from *The Three Stooges*, we both grappled unceremoniously with the rake, the bag, and the mighty serpent. Finally, in an act of complete bravery, Anthony grabbed the snake by its tail and together we dropped the monster into the bag and tied a knot in the top.

I looked over at Bob, feeling like a young warrior who had just passed his initiation into manhood and who had saved his tribe.

"Deadly right, Bob! A man killer!" I said.

"Nah," said Bob, chuckling to himself. "She's just a slow old woman. She has no teeth…completely harmless…ha ha ha. You were never in danger. I was only worried about the toddlers." I joined Bob in laughter, feeling a sense of accomplishment, nevertheless. Although the snake might have been harmless, my fear was certainly real.

Bob phoned the local snake handler who came out to pick it up and return it to its natural environment. When he opened the bag and looked inside he, said, "Wow, that's the biggest I've ever seen." Bob agreed. In all his time living on this land, he had never seen a snake as big as this.

"Who caught him?" the ranger asked. The proud warrior rose up in me. A city slicker at heart, I still felt pride knowing that together with my trusty companion, I had caught the mighty serpent—teeth or no teeth.

"We did," I happily replied, with my arm around Anthony.

Before settling in for the night, Bob suggested that the appearance of the snake was no accident. He said it was a good sign, probably sent from the rock. There we were, sharing stories all night about the mighty serpent snake and suddenly it appears from the darkness to join our group.

"No," Bob repeated for emphasis, "it was no accident." That night, before going asleep, I thought again about our collective voices and our connection to the land. Was it, after all, just a coincidence that this massive snake had appeared while we were talking about the Rainbow Serpent? I took it as a good sign, knowing we were at a sacred place. I closed my eyes and slowly drifted off into my own "dreamtime."

I woke the next morning feeling more alive than ever. As I looked out of the small window, I smiled and said "good morning" to the rock, which was once again bathing in a warm orange glow from the morning light. After breakfast, we drove to the rock and were met by one of the local female park rangers, who would escort us around for the next two days. Although Bob was a traditional owner of the land, it was still a requirement for film crews to have a ranger with us at all times.

Grace, a lovely blonde Australian girl from Sydney in her mid-thirties, had been at Uluru only for a few years. She instantly fell in love with Bob and was happy to take a back seat as she joined us in listening to Bob's dreamtime stories about Uluru and the Rainbow Serpent. We spent most of the day filming with Bob. During the breaks, Grace told us about how her life had changed in many unusual ways since she had arrived at Uluru. She told us how she had witnessed many tourists break down in tears during their brief time in the presence of this sacred rock.

"This place changes people," she said. "It has a healing energy about it that I can't explain." I looked over at Bob. With a knowing smile, he gently turned away and began to lead us to another part of this magical place.

I felt it too—the special energy. It reminded me of times I had spent in the stillness of the forest around the Margaret River house. But the energy at Uluru was more profound. It found you and embraced you whether you were looking for it or not. It allowed you to feel forgiveness for anyone who had ever troubled you in life. I experienced a sense of letting go of anger and resentment. In its place, a deep sense of love and gratitude filled my heart. I did my best to capture the quality of this sacred place through the lens of my camera. However, deep down I knew you had to be there to get the full experience.

The next day, with Grace in tow, we drove the 35 kilometres to our final destination. Kata Tjuta, meaning "many heads" to the Aboriginal people, is a group of more than thirty rounded red conglomerate masses of rock rising about 200 metres above the ground. Some of the rocks are bunched close together with only narrow, precipitous crevices between them. Just like their neighbour Uluru, these rocks have been sacred to the Aboriginal people since time immemorial, and figure prominently in their legends about the Dreaming, the time of creation.

As Grace guided us through the well-worn walkways between the huge rock faces, I asked her more about the energy in this area and what effects she had witnessed—especially on people. However, instead of calling her by her name, for some strange reason I called out "Emily." She responded nevertheless, and I thought how strange I had used a completely different name. We talked about her role as ranger and how she felt bad that many people chose to walk on top of Uluru even though the Aboriginal people requested them not to. Grace and Bob together explained that many white people have climbed the rock and that many have died doing so. The Aboriginal people are afraid that many more may also die, and to keep tourists safe, they have asked that no one climb the rock. Bob also explained the real gift of this place came from the walk around the bottom, not the climb above.

At the end of the day, I had one final question for Grace, but once again I called her "Emily." I immediately apologised.

She looked at me, smiling, and said, "Yes, that's the third time today you have called me Emily."

"I am sorry," I apologised again. "I have no idea why."

"I know," she said. "Emily is my real name, the name I was born with. As an adult, I changed it to Grace for personal reasons. No one has called me Emily for a long, long time." Her response took me aback, and we both looked up at the great rock faces towering over us.

"It's this place," she continued. "It does strange things to people. It connects us in a special way. Our subconscious communicates at a deeper level and we pick up on things that normally we miss because the busyness of city life distracts us. I wasn't surprised when you used my birth name—a sure sign that this place is having the right effect on you."

I looked over to Bob and Andrew; they knew it, too. From the moment he arrived, Andrew had felt a deep connection to the land and our small group. This was indeed a special place, and having me along as the cameraman meant a lot to him.

"You know, Darrell," he said, "when Jeremy recommended you as the cinematographer for this shoot, it wasn't so much your cinematic skills I was interested in. I was more interested in you as a person—what you believed in, what is inside your heart and how connected you are to this subject matter. Jeremy said you were definitely the guy for the job. As soon as we met, I knew he was right."

On the red gravel road back to the camp, I sat silently in the back seat of our four-wheel-drive, looking out the window as we headed back to Uluru. Andrews's words had meant a lot to me. He was right: I certainly felt a deep connection to the subject matter. Our evening conversations had not only proven we were all on the same page, but had also exposed my own passion for the way in which we raise children and connect them to the land. Although we had a healthy respect for each other professionally, our open conversations about life and its meaning made all the difference, connecting us at a deeper level. Friendships like these are special; some come to us once in a lifetime. I looked around at the people in the truck and once again I felt grateful for the voices that continued to show up in my life.

On the final morning, we got up before sunrise and followed Bob as he took a group of tourists to a small rise just west of Uluru. Positioned between the rock and where the sun was about to appear over the horizon, I filmed Bob leading the group through an ancient ceremony intended to connect them to this spiritual place. First, he asked them to turn to the North, then South, then East, and finally face West. Each time, the participants asked for forgiveness, allowing the spiritual energy from this sacred land to run through them. I filmed as grown men stood quietly with tears running down their faces. Such was the magnitude of Bob's prayer: it resonated through the bodies of everyone present. How could anyone not be touched by the moment?

In presence of this sacred site, and with a man who embodied all the grace and wisdom of an ancient time, I filmed the final few frames. Now completely silhouetted by the hot red golden sun, Bob held his hands in prayer. With eyes closed, he humbly gave thanks to the sacred rock. We all connected to something greater than any of us could have imagined.

As I packed the final camera case in the back of the 4WD, I felt a touch of sadness that our time together had come to an end. I began walking back to have one final check of the caravan when Andrew came storming out of the house toward me. Holding a cup of coffee in his left hand, he grabbed my shoulder with his right and stood only inches from my face. He stared straight into my eyes in a way that implied he didn't want me to miss what he was about to say.

"You *have* to write your book!" he insisted. "Everything you have told me over the past few days is so important to men today. The stories you told me about your boys, your passion for being a great father…men need to hear all these things, Darrell. They need a voice, and yours is a good one."

Andrew's words went right through me as though every cell off my body opened up in a way I hadn't felt for years. That's what happens when someone speaks directly to your soul. It's an incredible feeling, and one that I knew would change my life.

I gave Andrew a hug and then said goodbye to the rest of the group. I knew that, as soon as I got back to Perth, it was time to finish writing a book I started many years ago.

As I looked out the airplane window one final time at Uluru, now tinted deep red from the blazing sun above, it slowly drifted away into the distance. Andrew's words rang loud in my ear and the vision of Bob in full prayer silhouetted by the red hot sun was burned into my memory forever. I reached across and closed the blind on the oval window, with a deep knowing that my life would never be the same again.

In loving memory of "Uncle" Bob Randall

20

A BIGGER CONNECTION

As the boys got older I use to talk to them about some of the incredible things that had happened in my life. Things that to this day I still find hard to explain and yet I am convinced that once understood can bring massive success to people's lives. I hoped they would find the special messages in these stories that would eventually empower them in years to come....

Two significant life events happened to me within a few years of each other that convinced me of my connection to something greater than me. Though different, both reminded me of a voice that's more universal than the one we carry inside us. By tuning into this voice, I think we could forever change the way we raise our children.

In a previous chapter, I wrote about my trip to London to study with NLP founder John Grinder. However, I left out an important part of that story. It started three weeks earlier, when I got a phone call from a local producer in Perth.

"Hi Darrell, Laurel here. How's your day going?" She had called to see if I was available for an overseas assignment—something that sounded exciting and I was keen to take on. "How would you like to go to Libya to shoot an interview with Gaddafi?"

"Absolutely," I replied without hesitation. "When would we leave?"

An opportunity like this comes along once in a lifetime. Although I knew little about the man, I realised that the invitation of a Western crew to interview him was a rare opportunity indeed.

However, my excitement was short lived. Laurel then explained that the trip would need to happen in exactly three weeks, the same time I had booked to be in London. I guess it wasn't meant to be.

"Wow, that's a shame," Laurel said. "No problem, I'll give Kip a ring and see if he's available."

Kip was available and so was Jeremy—my close friend and sound recordist. Together, they and Laurel would travel to Libya and complete the assignment. Three of my good friends would set off on this Middle East adventure, while I would be left behind.

As I was about to hang up, I'll never forget what Laurel said next.

"Damn, it's such a shame you can't make it. But, hey, we're coming through London for one night on the way home. Maybe we'll see you there!"

"Sure, maybe," I replied, with a laugh.

Although missing out on the trip to Libya was disappointing, my trip to London to train with John Grinder, as I described earlier, was just as amazing. From the moment I landed, it was go, go, go. I arrived at 4.00 AM, took a train from the airport, and dragged my suitcase through the cobbled streets of a city that constantly reminded me of the game of Monopoly I played as a young boy. I loved to travel, and any hardship along the way was always brushed aside by a sense of gratitude for being somewhere in this world I had never been before.

I arrived at my hotel at six in the morning, only to find it didn't open for another three hours. When you travel on a budget, these things tend to happen. I sat on my suitcase as the sun began to rise between two distant buildings, and I watched as the cold streets of London began a new day. At 9.00 AM, the doors finally opened and I carried my bags up a flight of stairs to check in at the front desk.

"I'm sorry, sir, but your room won't be ready until 2.00 PM." Not the greeting I expected. After arranging to leave my suitcase with them, I decided to take a walk through the busy streets until my room was ready. When I finally got in, I set my alarm for two hours and crashed on the bed. The workshop with John began at 5.00 that afternoon, so I had little time to catch up on sleep.

Nearly all my time in London was taken up by the workshop, dinners with friends, and a trip back to the house I was born in. Thirty years ago, I had left England for the port of Fremantle, and this was my very first trip home. On my final day in London, I took the Underground to a small town called Southgate, about seven stops out of the city centre. I searched for the street I had grown up in, following a hastily-scribbled map concocted in my hotel room. My memory of my boyhood was vague. Because my parents had split up soon after we arrived in Australia, I had few opportunities for conversations about life in our London home. Nevertheless, I was determined to see the house. Maybe something would come flying back to me, a memory of my childhood, perhaps of happier times when Mum and Dad were still married, such as making snowballs with my brother and sister in the street; or maybe a voice from my childhood, a clue to how I came to be who I am today; or perhaps a loving conversation between my parents before their world fell apart.

The more I walked along the lonely streets, the more isolated I felt. Where was everyone? The streets were deserted. I kept walking, following the map until I finally found my old street. I counted the house numbers as I got closer to our old home. I tried to imagine what this street must have looked like to me as a toddler. No parks, no trees, no swings. No kids playing. Just rows of old terraced houses lined up one after the other under a drab overcast sky.

When I arrived at "my" house, I stood across the road and stared at the blue front door. Old memories came back to me, flickering like faded images: a photograph taken at this front door a few days before we left for Australia; me jumping into my mother's arms as she caught me in mid-air while my dad embraced my brother and sister, laughing at my antics—all moments in time when my childhood voices would have sounded so sweet.

I approached the door and knocked on the blue timber frame, waiting to see if anyone would answer. No one did. I pressed my ear against the door and even tried to sneak a peek through the window. What if someone did open the door? I hadn't given any real thought to what I was going to say. I just wanted to see who was living in my old house. What were their lives like? What had I missed out on?

A woman walking her dog on the other side of the road caught my attention. I crossed the street to talk to her. I could see right away that I had startled her. I put my hand out as a gesture of good will and said a friendly hello, mentioning why I was there. She told me she had lived in this area her whole life and that she had watched with sadness as it had deteriorated over the years. I asked why the streets were so empty, and she told me that most people didn't feel safe to walk around the streets anymore.

"It won't stop me though," she said defiantly. "Once the foreigners moved in, most of the locals were forced out. Your mum and dad did well to get out when they did."

I found it disappointing she felt that way, and wondered why we humans often struggle to assimilate. However, as I looked around at this bleak and seemingly unfriendly environment, I began to think she was right.

"There's no use knocking on that door over there either," she continued, pointing at my old house. "They wouldn't answer to a stranger even if they were home!" Her comments saddened me. Perhaps my parents had made the right decision to leave. I just didn't know why it all fell apart so quickly once they got to Australia.

As I started to leave, I looked back with a final glance at the house I barely knew. I listened for the echoes of laughter from that little boy who jumped into his mum's arms. I took solace in the fact that at least, if just for that one moment, happiness once lived here.

I grabbed the next train ride back to London were I was to spend my last evening before heading north to Leeds to finish my training. I had just a couple of places left to see on my list before I went back to the hotel. I had scheduled a lot and planned things as best I could to fit it all in. Although it was barely 5:00 PM, the daylight had almost gone. The neon signs in the centre of London now illuminated the encroaching darkness. As I walked out of Covent Garden, I stopped at the crosswalk and stared at the butcher's shop across the road. A feeling I can't explain came over me at that moment.

For the last five days, I knew exactly where I was going and what I had to do, but now it was different. Something felt strange. I stood there almost frozen, trying to think of why I was here. What was I was meant to do? Why couldn't I cross the road? Then, suddenly, it happened. A hand slapped me on the back, and as I turned around, I heard Laurel's voice.

"I told you we would see you in London!!" Laurel, Jeremy, and Kip were standing right behind me. They had just arrived that day and were in London for one night. Eight million people in the city, and I ran into them in that very spot!

Just when it seemed life couldn't get any stranger, I heard another voice.

"Laurel You're here!" I recognised the voice and turned to see a good friend running up to give us all a big hug. Carol, who worked in the film industry back in Perth, had "miraculously" appeared at this same moment in time and space.

After giving the guys a hug, she turned to me with an even more surprised look and said, "I didn't know Darrell was going to be here." At that point, I became even more confused.

"Okay, what's going on here?" I asked.

"You're never going to believe this," said Laurel. "Carol has been travelling around the world for the past year and rang me just before we left Perth for Libya. When she found out we were going to be in London for one night, it just so happened that it fit in perfectly with her own schedule. Before we left Perth, we made an agreement. 'Let's all meet at 5.00 PM at the crosswalk in front of Covent Garden on Monday, July 3."

"You mean Darrell isn't travelling with you guys?" Carol asked, clearly surprised.

"No. We saw him just before you arrived!"

I spent the rest of the night partying with my friends, catching up and finding out about everyone's trips. I never really spoke about my reasons for being in London, and for a while I forgot about the incredible coincidence that had brought us all together. But as I sat on the bus to Leeds the next morning, staring out the window at the never-ending grey flats and overcast sky, I couldn't help but think back to that moment on the crosswalk. What held me back from crossing the road? A voice perhaps? Or someone trying to get a message to me? Had I somehow tapped into a thought in tune with my own? How did I know to be there at that exact time? Was it just a coincidence? I mean…really? As I pondered this bizarre event, I remembered another earlier experience that had also made me question the unseen forces that seem to guide events in life.

I had received a call asking me if I could fly to Batam, the largest city on the northernmost tip of Indonesia, famous for its shipyards and steel manufacturing. I had been assigned to film the "load out" of a massive steel construction frame on to a huge barge, which was to be towed down to the oil fields off the northern coast of Western Australia. This one-off event had to be captured, and I was sent up there to shoot both stills and video.

Not until I was about to leave for the airport did I realise just how much equipment I would need. As a freelance cameraman, I was used to travelling with lots of luggage, but usually I would shoot only video. On this occasion, however, my client wanted me to also shoot still photographs—adding extra bags, a lot for one person alone to travel with.

When I arrived in Singapore, I had to grab two trolleys for all the gear. Walking out of the airport, the stifling humidity that comes with the afternoon rain immediately hit me. As sweat ran down my forehead, I could hardly wait to load all the gear into a taxi and crank up the air-conditioning. As I looked at the rows and rows of little blue Singapore taxis, I knew that none of them would be big enough to take eight large cases. Then I noticed a white taxi way off in the distance. I could just make out the shape of one of those old English taxis, a little bigger than the local ones. I left the cases behind and ran to grab the "London" cab. I opened the door, hopped in and motioned to the driver to move forward. As we came alongside the gear, I told him to stop so I could grab my luggage.

He didn't realise I had so much gear and told me the cab didn't have room for it all, and that I needed to get a second taxi. I never split my gear when I travel, having heard some scary stories of guys losing half their equipment from doing that. I told him to leave it to me. The old English taxi had "suicide" doors that opened outward from the middle. I managed to pack all eight cases inside the back of the cab until they almost touched the roof. The driver complained that he couldn't see behind him. I told him, with a smile, that it was fine because we were only going forward.

Only when he asked where we were headed did I finally check my schedule. To my surprise, I realised I didn't have much time to catch the ferry leaving for Batam. My tight schedule left me ninety minutes between landing at Singapore airport and making my way to the ferry. It would take at least 45 minutes to get to the port, my driver told me, because of peak traffic. I had already taken quite a bit of time sorting my gear, so I suggested he get a move on and not spare the horses.

This filming assignment came at a time when I was reading a lot about the power of intention—in books by Wayne Dyer, Abraham Hicks, and Gregg Braden. Gregg's *The Isaiah Effect* talked about the prophet Isaiah, and how ancient Essenes had part-authored the famous *Dead Sea Scrolls*. According to Gregg, even though nearly 800 scrolls had been discovered, only one—written by Isaiah—remains intact. This ancient scroll now resides at the Shrine of the Book at the Israel Museum in Jerusalem. Because it's so rare and valuable, the Isaiah scroll sits displayed in a bulletproof glass cylinder in the middle of the room. In order to protect it for the ages, the display column retracts into a reinforced concrete and steel chamber designed to withstand a nuclear attack.

What on Earth is written on that scroll to make it so valuable? Although Gregg explains why in his book, I got a fuller explanation in person a few years later during our trip in Tibet. Surrounded by the mountains in this spiritual land, he told us how the ancient Essenes thrived around the time of Christ. Known for their unorthodox practices, this nomadic Jewish sect of poets, mystics, and alchemists lived mainly on the outskirts of the cities. They wrote about the ability to turn water into wine.

Many scholars believe that Jesus was an Essene initiate who often attended their secret meetings. Although the *Isaiah Scroll* describes many strange or miraculous phenomena, at its heart it delivers a special kind of prayer. Gregg wanted us to focus on this. He explained that all prayer is sacred and that everyone has the right to pray in his or her own way.

He pointed out that most people pray for something they don't yet have, and that by doing so they energize the very thing they don't want to experience. According to Gregg, the Essenes realised that the power of prayer comes from *feeling* the outcome of what you pray for as if it already exists. That feeling then resonates out into the universe and puts in motion a process that will bring the exact result you pray for. The challenge for most of us is to realistically create that feeling and then sustain it for long enough without reverting back to the feeling of the reality we currently find ourselves in.

I'm sure some people will find this idea a bit of a stretch. But, as I have said before, scientific research now supports the idea that intentions do have power to change or redirect how reality unfolds—confirming ancient wisdom. You can test this for yourself by starting with small intentions and see what happens. Gregg suggests that over the centuries—between the time of the Essenes and today—we seem to have lost access to a "technology" that has always resided inside us—something I was about to put to a massive test.

When the taxi pulled up at Singapore's bustling harbourfront precinct, about 20 meters from the ferry to Batam, I looked at my watch...wow! We made it with just 15 minutes to spare. I unloaded my luggage and paid the driver. As he sped away, I turned to see a solid, dark-skinned gentleman wearing some kind of maritime uniform at the entrance to the ferry. I took out my ticket and asked if he had some kind of trolley I could use to carry my equipment onto the ferry.

With a wry smile, he shook his head, and said, "No, I don't."

"Well then," I asked, "could you please give me a hand to get my luggage on board?" He took a couple of steps closer to inspect my bags and said something that was about to throw my world into chaos.

"I'm sorry, sir, but those cases are not coming on this ferry; and at this point in time, neither are you!"

"Why on Earth not?" I exclaimed in shock.

"Because neither you nor your luggage have gone through customs."

Then it suddenly dawned on me: Batam is part of Indonesia and this is *Singapore*. Even though Batam was just a short ferry ride away, I still had to go through immigration and customs. I looked around the busy harbour and asked, "Where the heck is customs?"

He pointed off into the distance, about 400 meters away to a multi-storeyed shopping mall. "Up there, on the top floor."

For some strange reason, the immigration office was located on the top floor of a shopping mall. Here I was with eight pieces of heavy luggage, no trolley, and just over ten minutes to get all of it up through customs and back down onto the ferry—in a word: *impossible*. I sat down next to my pile of gear as my frustration and anxiety mounted. This one-off assignment for a very important client could not be repeated. So much depended on me. I just had to catch that ferry. Without any logical way of making the impossible happen, I decided to do something I had never done before.

I sat still, almost motionless, turned my attention inside myself, and—dare I say it—*prayed*. But not the usual kind of prayer that pleads for something I didn't have. Sitting there on the dock, I prayed the way the ancient Essenes did. *I felt to the core of my being that I was already on that ferry.*

Everything Gregg had spoken about came flooding back. I began to imagine what it would be like to get on that ferry. I felt the feeling of relief that would surround me after making it happen. All the while, I repeated, "Please bring to me the people, resources and events that will allow me to get on this ferry and travel now to the island of Batam."

My inner voice drifted out into the universe, connecting me to the wisdom of the ages, as I sat in silence waiting for my miracle to happen.

And it did.

At that moment, I suddenly felt compelled to open my eyes. As I looked up, the thick bustling crowd in front of me parted like the red sea. From the mall entrance, a man appeared and made a beeline straight toward me. As he got closer, I saw he was pushing an upright trolley used for carting boxes of vegetables. His van was parked in the loading zone directly behind my pile of luggage, and he came right up to me.

"Hey there!" I yelled, "I don't know where you came from or who sent you, but I'm so glad you're here. I'm in desperate need of you and your trolley. I have ten minutes to get this pile of luggage up through customs and onto this ferry and you are my only hope. I am happy to pay you for your help."

He looked at me with the most beautiful warm smile. "Of course, I can!" Immediately, he began loading as many cases onto his trolley as he could manage. I followed, carrying the rest of my bags, and we both rushed as fast as we could to the door he had magically come through at the bottom of the shopping mall.

He had a special key that gave us access to the goods lift, which meant we didn't have to travel with the shoppers, or stop at any of the floors on the way up. When we reached the customs level, he took me straight to the front of the line. He spoke to the officials in Bahasa, and obviously said something about the urgency of my situation. My passport was immediately stamped and my luggage hastily shuffled through the x-ray machines. Back on the trolley, we exited down the same lift, out the service door, and arrived back at the ferry just as the ferryman was about to pull the platform away from the jetty.

He looked at me once again with that wry smile, but this time, after seeing the appropriate tags on my luggage, offered to help. We both loaded the gear off the trolley and onto the waiting ferry. I put my hand into my pocket and pulled out a U.S. $50 dollar bill. I wanted to repay the courier who had been sent to my aid by the voices from above. But as I turned to pass the money to this stranger with a trolley who had amazingly come into my life, he jumped back into his van and drove away as mysteriously as he had arrived.

Without even the chance to thank him, let alone give him some money, he vanished into a sea of people that once again closed in between us, leaving me to simply sit and wonder about what had just transpired.

As the ferry pulled away from the port, I sat watching a spectacular magenta sunset cast a warm glow over the bustling city of Singapore. My thoughts quickly turned to the man who had just come into my life at the exact time I needed him. *How did that just happen?* I wondered. Did I make it happen? And if so, *how*—with my voice, my thoughts, my intention, my *feelings?* Perhaps I was reading way too much into what was simply a highly unlikely coincidence. Wayne Dyer once said, "Your life starts to get interesting when you begin to manage the coincidences in your life." Now I began to understand what he meant.

I have often reflected on two astounding "coincidences" in my life—one on the streets of London and the other on the Singapore harbor—moments when a doorway to other possibilities, to another domain of reality, opened up for me. These kinds of events happen for most us at one time or another. However, many dismiss them as mere happenstance. I can't help but think that Gregg Braden is probably right. Perhaps we all do possess an inner "technology" that modern civilisation is just beginning to understand.

In 2005, not long after these events occurred, and on my return to Perth, I decided to look for evidence to further support my theory of our deep and universal interconnection. After studying the works of Gregg Braden and many other great thinkers, I ended up designing and running a one-day workshop called "Creating Your Destiny." Thirty people filled a lecture room I had rented from a local university, and I took them through the theory and practice of what I had uncovered through my research.

Here are the basic principles, based on insights from various luminaries of our time:

In his acceptance speech for the 1918 Nobel Prize for Physics, Max Planck, who discovered the quantum, stunned his colleagues by saying, "As a man who has spent my whole life studying matter I can tell you this much...there is no matter as such. Our world is made up of succeedingly smaller patterns of vibratory fields, nestled one within another within another, and beneath these fields we must assume that there is an intelligence or a mind and we call that creative force God."

Planck and other physicists tell us that when we reach into the subatomic world, the laws of classical physics break down and something else begins to happen. *Something else exists besides matter.* When we create, heart-based feelings and emotions inside our bodies change our DNA and produce quantum effects beyond our bodies. These effects change our physical world. If we don't understand how this works, when certain events occur in our lives, we might dismiss them as coincidence or even miracles. When we *do* understand, however, we begin to access a powerful inner technology that connects matter and mind, energy and consciousness in ways that empower us to intentionally change the world.

Ancient traditions have spoken about a power that resides in everyone—an inner technology more powerful than most of us yet realise. Across the globe, scholars and researchers continue to discover and decode messages handed down through the centuries. Some of these messages come to us in languages we are just beginning to understand. However, we already know from the fragments we have deciphered that these ancient messages talk about accessing and harnessing creative universal forces beyond the reach of modern science.

Nevertheless, Western science has made great advances in understanding how the human brain functions. From this research, we now know that how we think and program ourselves to respond to life events makes a major difference to our ultimate success or failure. I invite you to consider the possibility that each of us contains ancient memories of a highly sophisticated "inner technology" we call prayer. We can express the creative potential of this technology through the power of intention, coupled with coherent connections between our thoughts, feelings, and emotions. The true power of this prayer lies not in our heads but in our hearts.

When you focus on cultivating the power of intention, you can align with the ever-evolving creative forces of the universe. Doing so, you have the power to *co-create your destiny!*

* * *

I sometimes think about Mark, the young trainee camera assistant who came into my life so many years ago. Mark clearly had a huge desire to succeed in life. He had a passion for his camerawork that spoke powerfully to the creative forces around him.

Was it purely a coincidence that so many opportunities kept flooding his way until ultimately he got to the place where he was living his dream? How did a young kid from Perth rise to be one of the best in the world in his chosen field? Mark carried inside him an intention—a deep inner voice—that reached out and dialogued with the world around him, shaping it to align with his goals. He matched this voice of intention with a certainty about where he was headed. This, in turn, guided him to pick the right heroes to listen to. He found his own voice, in perfect harmony with the universal voice—the ultimate secret to success.

As I write these words, I feel a desire to make this book a great success. That feeling already resides inside me, speaking loudly to the creative forces around us. In doing so, I know I am beginning to attract into my life everything I require to make this book the beginning of a dream I have always held: to be a successful author and speaker.

No matter how old you are or what has happened in your past, you always have choice-points in your life—moments when you can change your destiny forever. It's never too late to break away from the limiting voices of your past and surge forward with renewed optimism about what's possible for your future. Perhaps it's time to create a new voice, a powerful voice that will become your guide and mentor for the next step of your journey. Be brave and courageous and make this new voice your constant companion. I promise you the universe will always listen and respond to the voice that resonates loudest from within your heart.

In doing this, of course, we model for our children that anything is possible—*provided you intend it clearly and powerfully enough*. We can tell our children what we want them to hear; ultimately, who we are and who we become speaks to them the loudest.

The next step in the evolution of our species depends on how we raise our children. Let's give them the gift of learning to listen to and trust their own inner voices, encouraging them to dialogue with the silent, ever-powerful Voice of the Ultimate.

21

A PARENTAL EVOLUTION

As babies, we come into this world with a clean sheet—a blank canvass on which we can paint the most glorious of lives imaginable. Infinite potential and possibilities surround us every moment of our existence. And yet for so many...their wildest of dreams soon fade into quiet lives of desperation. The world is filled with the lost potential of adults who gave up on their dreams, people who never found their true purpose and silently passed away, no doubt wishing things could have been different. Wayne Dyer often said, "Don't die with your music in you...for the world needs to hear you sing."

What stops us from reaching our true potential in life?

Throughout this book, I have echoed the many voices that played their parts in my journey from a boy to a man; perhaps more important, from a son to a father. Like many, I struggled to find the right voice to guide me. I tried my best to separate the words of wisdom from the constant chatter of a crowded life. Earlier, I wrote that Warren Buffet once said, "You're lucky in life if you pick the right heroes." Taking his cue, in these pages, I have introduced you to many of the heroes who have influenced my life. Although I had a difficult childhood, I still consider my mother and father among my heroes.

I have learned in life that everyone does the best they can, given their circumstances. Sometimes the people who hurt you the most turn out to be your greatest gifts. With the wisdom of age, you can look back over the years at the moments that challenged you most. Perspective reveals how they made you who you are today; every scar can serve as a reminder of healed wounds and a battle well fought. Such moments eventually define who we are in the ultimate journey toward finding our own true voice.

As you go through life, listen for the voices that will get you to your next destination. Sometimes, hearing them can be a challenge. Every now and then we need to stop and take stock of our life. Where to now? What to do next?

Howard Thurman once wrote, "Don't ask what the world needs. Ask what makes you come alive, and go do that. Because what the world needs is people who have come alive."

If you listen carefully, the voice you need to hear may drift in on a summer's breeze, float across a sunset lake, or whisper in the rustle of leaves. Like a long lost friend, the voice you require may arrive in ways most unexpected. As a young boy, I struggled with the voices that impacted me from my home environment. Over time, however, I met mentors—sometimes even strangers—whose wisdom guided me each step of my journey. Hearing these different voices, I eventually found my own voice and began to trust it more than any other.

While writing this book, it often dawned on me that perhaps what the world needs now more than anything else is a way of raising our children so *they* don't have to recover from their childhood.

Dr Shefali Tsabary, a wonderfully insightful clinical psychologist, sums it up well:

> *Ultimately, our children will internalize the voices of their parents and these voices become the blueprint of who they will eventually become. As parents, few hold a greater power or more immense a responsibly over how our children turn out. Perhaps it's time we occupy the role of parenthood in an entirely different way. With a renewed curiosity, a heightened awareness and a transformed commitment. It's our collective parenting that needs to be at the forefront of our global consciousness. It is the call, the lynch pin that affects how our children will thrive.*
>
> *Everything—how our children take care of themselves, each other, the Earth, show compassion, tolerate differences, handle their emotions, create, invent, innovate—this is where global transformation begins. We cannot expect our children to embody an enlightened consciousness if we as parents haven't dared to model this ourselves. It all starts with us and how we parent. Our children are facing challenges today that we couldn't have dreamed of, and evidence suggests they are buckling under the pressure. Depression, anxiety, suicide, and a generation of medicated children are now becoming the norm.*

Something is amiss. We need to sit up, pay attention and raise our children differently. Now of course, parental influence isn't the only factor at play. There are confusing and colliding and chaotic influences in our children's lives that shape them indeterminately.

There's neurobiology, temperament, social pressures, and poverty. We could blame psychiatry, education, big pharma, and the government ... and chances are we could be right. But our influences in this sphere are relatively limited. But let me tell you where we hold indubitable power. That is in the relationship we nurture with our children. Our children and us—moment after moment. Nothing glamorous here; early in the morning as they brush their teeth, as we comb their hair, as we wipe away their tears, take away their fears, and kiss them goodnight. This is where each one of us holds transformative power.

Parental evolution is the solution. The extent to which we as parents know ourselves is the extent to which our children will. The extent to which we as parents can love deeply, laugh loudly, risk bravely, and lose freely, is the extent to which our children will know joy and freedom. The extent to which we can run out into the rain without fear of getting wet is the extent to which our children will live lives of courage. The time to awaken is now. The parenting paradigm needs to shift. No more the parent as the greater than, but now we need to look at our children as equal, if not greater transforming agents. Our children are our awakeners. They are our teachers.

It is time for us parents to answer the call, to pause, to reflect more and to connect to our own abundance. To trust our children and understand their brilliance. To follow their lead, to self-love, to create purpose, to enter worth, to be in gratitude. For this is how our children will absorb wholeness and abundance, fullness and spirit. And from this place they can fly free. It is time for us parents to answer the call to our own awakening. The moment is now and our children await.

* * *

I have tried in this book to shine a light specifically on the importance of fatherhood. I have shared some ideas on what worked for me—hoping they might be useful to anyone thinking of taking this wonderful journey.

Now going on sixteen, my boys will soon be getting their drivers' licenses and heading off on their own life journeys. The tiny frail bodies, so soft and subtle as little children, are now tall, strong, and hardened with time. However, although their external frames have changed greatly, I feel their hearts have remained the same. As their father, I still hug them as tightly now as I did back then. A handshake just won't do. I still kiss them goodnight and tell them how much I love them, every day.

Those big bright eyes and beautiful smiles still remind me how lucky I am to be a dad. I know I can't get back those early years: changing their nappies and washing those tiny little bums; waking up on Christmas morning to see if Santa and his reindeer had come; climbing up into the tree house and watching the world go by; hearing them coming home from school, and then feeling them thunder into my arms.

And yet...it is soon to be no more.

A home without children can be a quiet, lonely place. It's not something I like to think about. I imagine such times of transition can be difficult for many parents; a sense of loss and the sadness of a wonderful time now gone forever. Lounge rooms and hallways filled with the photographs of family picnics help to stop it all from becoming a faded memory.

Even today, I can still hear the distant echoes of laughter from Cody and Taylor, chasing each other down the hallway as fast as their little legs could take them. I can see it as clearly as if it all happened just yesterday. Is this what lies ahead for us? In some ways it doesn't seem fair.

And yet I always knew this time was inevitable. I guess that's why I didn't want to miss any of it. Earlier, I said that my boys were like oxygen to me; I needed them to breathe. Maybe that's why the thought of them not being around begins to tighten around my neck. Was I—am I—too attached? Can I love too much?

They say we hold our children's hands for a while but hold their hearts for eternity. This thought warms my own heart and allows me to breathe a bit easier. I think of the many great years ahead and the possibility of grandchildren. Surely I will still have much to contribute as a grandfather? Maybe that's another book. One I have yet to live.

I dearly hope that in raising our boys the way we did, Jules and I have given them both a childhood voice that will serve them well in later life. Understandably, there are no guarantees; but perhaps the constant loving voices of an adoring mother and a strong emotionally available doting father will be enough.

As parents, Jules and I were more than happy to be their "best bet."

For others, the voices missed in early childhood can show up later in ways they could never imagine. Certainly they did in my life. I sometimes think of Ray, the gaffa, who taught me about every light in his truck. I think of the boss who said I was an insurance risk and then gave me my first job. I think of the cowboy who taught me a thing or two about boys and horses, and the guy in London who demonstrated the power of language. Then there's the Aboriginal elder who spoke about our connection to the land. I think of the Tibetan monk who taught me about the science of compassion, and the mystic who commanded me to write this book...I think of my wife, Jules, who believed in me from the first day we met. All of these voices, and many more, have played their parts in the symphony of my life.

I think of two little boys with voices screaming as they ran toward me crying, "Daddy's home! Daddy's home!" and how those little voices inspired me to live the greatest life I could.

As a father of two young boys, I did my best to examine my own childhood and look at the things that didn't work. I am now grateful for all those experiences, and at the same time I have made a conscious choice to change the things that didn't work. Through it all, I also made sure I loved every minute of it.

In the end, it's not what happens to us in life that counts, but how we deal with it. As new parents, we not only have the responsibility but also the opportunity to make sure our own children have the greatest start to life we can give them. Mostly, this comes from bathing them in unconditional love.

Author Joseph Chilton Pearce once said, "I think we have the opportunity to eradicate all forms of violence from our world today if we simply understand the requirements of the first three years of a baby's life."

As parents, we are gatekeepers to a better world. Each of us can take a stand that says, "It ends with me!" No more can we afford to pass on to society or future generations the problems of a childhood gone wrong.

Take stock of your own childhood memories, find forgiveness for those who unintentionally hurt you the most, and love your children with all your heart. Find your voice, stand tall, and shout to the world.

The future is in our hands. "We are the ones we've been waiting for."

22

RECONNECTION

My father recently reached out to reconnect with me and the boys. We all now spend more time together, and I'm happy we are beginning to heal the past. A few weeks ago, on a warm Sunday afternoon, we sat under a tree watching Taylor and Cody play a game of cricket. We reminisced about old times and dear friends we hadn't seen since my childhood. I mentioned Sally, a close family friend who had two children roughly the same age as my sister and me. We often had picnics together when we were very young.

"Oh, Sally. Yes, yes, I remember," my dad remarked, smiling warmly. "I haven't seen her for nearly 30 years. She loved you kids and was so much fun to be around. I have no idea where she lives now. I often wonder what happened to her and what she's doing. I wonder if she even still lives in Australia."

One week later I was sitting under the same tree. This time, with my youngest boy, Taylor, who was once again playing cricket for his local club. During a break, he came over to sit with me and our golden retriever, Riley. Dad wasn't there that day.

Taylor was hungry, so I decided to drive off to buy him a sandwich, while he waited patiently with Riley. When I returned, I saw him chatting to a friendly-looking older lady, as her dog and Riley romped together. Taylor and the elderly lady seemed deep in conversation. I walked over to say hello.

"Is this your boy?" she asked lovingly.

"Yes," I replied.

"He's such a polite young boy. He was kindly taking the time to explain to me how one plays this confusing game." She looked over at Taylor as he played with the dogs. As if talking to herself I heard her whisper, "He's a beautiful boy."

As I listened, I noticed her slightly dishevelled hair and that her legs had weathered with time. I couldn't help thinking I had met her before. Although time ages us all, some characteristics stay with us forever. I knew I had heard that voice before, and had a strange and intuitive feeling that I knew this woman.

"Well, I best be on my way," she said, as she slowly began to meander off.

"Before you go," I yelled, "Do you mind if I ask your name?"

"Yes, my dear. It's Sally."

"Sally Reeba?" I couldn't hide my amazement.

"How on Earth did you know that?

"My name is Darrell Brown, You were a close friend of my father!"

"My God. I haven't seen him for a lifetime! How did you recognise me?"

We spoke for another ten minutes and swapped phone numbers. I told her that only a week ago, Dad and I had sat here under the same tree and reminisced about the times we all had spent together. I told her how Dad wondered whatever happened to her. Understandably, we were both astonished by the coincidence—or synchronicity—of meeting under the exact same tree a week after that initial conversation.

Sally's voice was one of my childhood echoes, and instantly brought back a flood of fond memories. I think all the voices of our childhood affect us. In a strange way, they stay with us forever. Although now an old lady nearing her eighties, Sally hardly resembled the woman I had known as a seven-year-old boy some forty years ago. And yet her voice remained a constant link between the past and the present. A warm feeling came over me as I watched her hobble away with her dog by her side. I looked over at Taylor and gave him a glowing smile. A voice from my childhood had now become a voice in his life, too—so strange, and yet so beautiful at the same time.

I couldn't help thinking about this moment. How many young boys fixated on a game of cricket would bother to turn around and not only answer an old lady's question, but also take the time to politely explain the rules of the game? Had he simply grunted or shrugged his shoulders, she would have kept going and our paths may never have crossed again.

I recalled the conversations we had in the treehouse when they were young: "Don't miss life, boys. Don't bury your head in those little screens, because you'll miss opportunities that life throws your way—unexpected chances to connect with people who can add to the symphony of voices from your childhood."

I watched as Taylor ran back to his teammates. He wasn't missing life. And me? Well, I certainly wasn't missing his.

AFTERWORD

I think one of the most powerful questions you can ever ask someone is – *Tell me about your father?* The way each of us responds to that question may tell us much about our childhood voices. I like to think that every father did the best he could to raise his children with the resources he had at the time. Writing this book has given me the opportunity to examine my own life and the relationship I had with my own father. I love my Dad very much and feel that this book has helped to heal my heart…perhaps even his. I look forward to the years we still have together.

My wider intention in writing this book was to remind us all of the vitally important role fathers play in their children's lives. I wanted to particularly highlight the need for fathers to be present and available during the pregnancy and first three years of their child's life. But perhaps more importantly I wanted to remind Dads everywhere of how much fun and laughter these early years can bring to your world. It should never be looked at as a chore but rather the happiest time of your life.

A strong loving father present in these years will impact in the most profound way imaginable and set up a bond between father and child that will never be broken. You are and always will be….Their "best bet."

Of course, to all the mothers – I'm not for a second suggesting your role isn't of equal importance, however I truly believe that it's the role of fatherhood that society has appeared to have lost in recent times.

People sometimes ask what successful parenting might look like. What do you look for in your children? How do you measure success? Is academic achievement the main focus? What about sporting ability? My children are very well behaved. They sit still and have good manners … is that it? Should they display good values or do volunteer work?

I think all these qualities are wonderful and certainly signs of a great home environment. However to be honest, the one thing we admired most about the boys may surprise some people. I don't think I've ever read about it in any parenting book, and yet I'm sure that if we could all guide our children in this one area, it would go a long way towards them living a fulfilled life.

The one thing our boys do well, without any encouragement from us, is connect in a very loving way with other people's young children. Whether they be nieces or nephews, the neighbour's kids, or even those of complete strangers. Nothing makes Jules and me more proud of our boys than the way they reach out and connect with these little toddlers – sometimes, even babies. Any child that can create a loving connection with another child, who genuinely loves playing with them, giving them a cuddle, making them laugh, or simply picking them up when they stumble over, is already showing signs of a quality that many people struggle with in their adult lives. The ability to love openly and unconditionally.

If young boys today are going to display these attributes then they must be modelled to them by their fathers. It's up to all Dads to break the shackles of the past and show our boys how to love openly, allow ourselves to be vulnerable and simply display our unconditional love for <u>all</u> the tiny feet that cross their paths.

When children can display this loving quality constantly and freely, it's a sure sign that they are on their way to living a very happy life and that their childhood voices are serving them well.

REFERENCES AND RESOURCES

Chapter 4

Pearce, Joseph Chilton., (2004), The Biology of Transcendence; Crack In The Cosmic Egg, Paperback ed., Park Street Press

Chapter 6

Pearce, Joseph Chilton., (2003), Magical Child Magical Parent, Suicide Statistics, page 85., North Atlantic Books and In Joy Publications

Pearce, Joseph Chilton., (2004), The Biology of Transcendence, Paperback ed., Park Street Press

Eldredge, John., (2001), Wild at Heart, Thomas Nelson Publishers.

Farrell, Warren,. (2013), National Men's Health Gathering Brisbane October 22nd – 25th.

Chapter 12

"Many Australian men also work longer hours than their counterparts in nearly all other developed countries". The Advertiser: Lauren Novak- Adelaide Now June 13, 2013

Chapter 16

The Notebook, (2004), Film, New Line Cinemas / Time Warner / Warner Bros Entertainment

Chapter 17

Neufeld, Gordon Ph.D. & Mate, Dr. Gabor M.D,. (2008) Hold on to your Kids, Ballantine Books Canada, ASIN B001LOEFZU.

Chapter 18

Millman, Dan., (1980). The Way of the Peaceful Warrior, HJ Kramer.

Chapter 21

Pearce, Joseph Chilton., (2004), What Babies Want Vol 1, Hana Peace Works.

Tsabary, Dr Shefali, TEDx San Francisco, June 2013

ACKNOWLEDGMENTS

To all the men who courageously guided me through life: who opened doors when there weren't any open, who whispered words of wisdom when I was in doubt and who picked me up when I stumbled.

These are some of those men–Ray Thomas, Ross MacDonald, Gary De Rodriguez, Ross Tinney, Don Shepherd, John Grinder, Andrew Harvey, Damian Pforr, Monty Roberts, Gregg Braden, Dad.

I also want to acknowledge the men of the North Beach Junior Football Club who joined me in raising strong-grounded boys with open loving hearts.

ABOUT THE AUTHOR,
DARRELL BROWN

Storyteller, Father, Pioneer…

Based in Perth Western Australia, Darrell Brown has spent the last 30 years travelling the world as a freelance cinematographer. Self driven and highly motivated, his passion for his work has given him a unique window into the world that few have rarely seen. Working for organisations such as 60 Minutes, The Lonely planet and Discovery Channel, as well as filming local, national and international TV commercials, Darrell has worked with Prime Ministers, Celebrities and Sporting Heroes the world over. This insightful perspective on life has given him a good understanding of how the world works and what is required to make a success of one's life.

Running parallel to this journey was Darrell's desire to immerse himself in the world of self-development. He trained in NLP (Neuro Linguistic Programming) and over a period of years became a Master practitioner and Associate trainer. He has travelled to all parts of the globe to train with some of the brightest minds on the planet and he has studied in Alpha Dynamics, Ericksonian Hypnosis, Avatar and much more.

However at the age of 35 Darrell became a father for the first time and as such his passion quickly changed to the raising of his two boys. With his loving wife by his side he asked himself a rare and unique question;

"What would it take to be the best father he could possibly be?"

With that he started studying and reading every parenting book he could find and enrolled in an online academy for parenting. His desire to be a completely hands on Dad and devote as much time as possible to being a father drew out of him the best of everything he had studied. His passion for fatherhood was equalled by the immense joy he received as he watched his two boys grow into young men.

Now at the age of 50 the culmination of his life's work has been turned into a wonderfully inspiring book "**Raised By Our Childhood Voices**".

This book has a simple message for Fathers everywhere – *that they are and must continue to be their children's "best bet" in life*.

At a time when our kids need us the most his concern is that Fathers have perhaps taken their eyes off the road. Our boys need strong men in their lives more than ever before. It's time for all fathers to spend quality time with their children, be emotionally available and consciously connect as deeply as possible with their boys.

Through the pages of this transformational book Darrell continues to prove that true wisdom will always come from the heart.

CONTINUE YOUR JOURNEY

As you come to the completion of this book you may wish to continue your journey of learning, exploring and discovery. I invite you to connect with me at www.darrellbrown.com.au/bookgifts, twitter account @_darrellbrown, Facebook - https://www.facebook.com/darrell.brown.944023 where you will also be able to access a wealth of free resources and information to do with what I have captured in this book.

They are designed to support you and to help you to become the sort of parent to your boys (and girls) that you dream to be.

PRAISE FOR RAISED BY OUR CHILDHOOD VOICES

"**Raised By Our Childhood Voices** is so much more than a book - it is a unique that takes one through one's own childhood in a gentle and reflective way. Darrell Brown has had one hell of a ride so far in his life and his life journey showed me the value of finding ones 'spark' as early as possible and to follow it with persistence and enthusiasm.

Darrell is a resilient man - a resilience learned through having a childhood with significant challenge and yet he does not let that define who he is or what he chooses to make of himself and his life.

As a former West Aussie I remember the story of the tree house and shared the exasperation of a world gone mad. His incredible passion for being the best dad possible while sharing himself as fully and honestly with the woman he loves is both touching and inspirational. Our world is a better place because of men like Darrell and I am a better person for having read his autobiographical book and it has given me hope and validates my belief that our greatest teachers teach wisdom from their heart with a good dose of humility."

Maggie Dent,
Australian Author, parenting and resilience educator.
Author of Saving our Children from Our Chaotic World,
Nurturing Kids' Hearts and Souls,
Real Kids in an Unreal World.

"Drawing on his own childhood with its ups and a lot of downs, diverse leaders on the field from Neuroscientists to 'Horse whisperers,' including Joseph Chilton Pearce, Bruce Lipton, Gordon Neufeld to NLP, Tony Robbins and many more, Darrell Brown in Raised by Our Childhood Voices weaves his passionate quest to be the best dad ever.

Definitely a male voice and with ruthless honesty he describes how becoming a parent is the most challenging developmental experience an adult can have - if they recognise the opportunity - which is implicit in the book's title, **Raised by Our Childhood Voices.** Down to earth and full with practical insights Darrell's well written story invites every guy to discover what he discovered, that nothing compares in importance or for one's personal growth to mentoring the next 'critical' generation of humanity, one kid at a time. I loved it and you will too."

Michael Mendizza;
Founder, Touch the Future,
Co Author - Magical Parent Magical Child

"**Raised by Our Childhood Voices**" is a fine book, moving, eloquent, packed with stories, confessions, deep and authentic spiritual information and discovery. It is both an enthralling and sometimes scoldingly honest memoir and a passionate plea to all men to uncover and live the deep brave love of their true nature. Here's hoping, dear Darrell, that this book will be the first of many, and that its many inspiring and helpful messages will reach as large an audience as possible.

Andrew Harvey;
Author - *The Hope* – And International speaker on Sacred Activism

"In this deeply personal and honest book, Darrell lays bare the power our childhood has over our adult life. To be read with an open heart and curious mind, this book will take you to your own past and dare you to heal the wounds that lie open."

Dr. Shefali Tsabary,
Author of New York Times Bestseller,
The Conscious Parent - "As seen on Oprah!"

"Training Youth Leadership in a variety of schools both in Australia and the USA I have always known that there has never been an owner's manual for raising children, but this is probably the best set of skills for parents I have ever read.

Written with open authenticity I was enthralled with the story and coupled with a masterful toolbox for parents, it is an amazing road map for raising thriving kids with self esteem. I highly recommend this book to anyone who requires insight, tools and systems to shine a light into the heart of what makes a great parent with successful children. Well done."

Gary De Rodriguez,
CEO Popleistic USA

Thanks for sending me your book. I loved reading it – the way the stories intertwine with your messages about child rearing work at many levels. You give the reader parenting wisdom, gained from your unique blend of travel, work, self-learning and your own history. You talk about courage and the warrior, and developing the parallel qualities of Artist and Warrior in boys.

I think the book will be a great seller. I wish you every success – it's been a long journey.

Donna Skender,
Creative Director: Lasso Productions and Mum

"We are in desperate need of a new vision for our men and boys that aligns with this astonishing, sometimes bewildering new world we inhabit. **Raised By Our Childhood Voices** offers profound and practical wisdom for everyone who seeks to nourish and empower this new generation of boys, who come to us full of unrealised potential.'"

Maggie Hamilton;
Author, *What Men Don't Talk About* and *What's Happening To Our Boys*

"Darrell – I am loving your book!!!! I read half of it the day I opened the book and couldn't put it down..... It's heartfelt and warm and is a true, honest account of your experience as a father....and most importantly you set the scene about your own childhood which I really enjoyed reading :))))...... You made me smile, laugh, cry, reminisce, contemplate life and think about my own son and how I am parenting him....and I'm only halfway!.... cannot wait to read the rest xxx"

Fenella Pecotich,
Senior Graphic Designer - New Mum

"Touching, tender, and tough, Darrell Brown gives us the full tour of his experience as both a child and a parent. Having learned to be self-reliant and not show his feelings as a teen, Brown walks us through his efforts to create connection, stability, and emotional awareness not only in his sons, but also in himself. Told with honesty, humor, and hubris, **Raised by Our Childhood Voices** gives us all a better understanding of what fatherhood can look like."

Andrew P. Smiler,
Author of "Dating and Sex: A Guide for the 21st Century Teen Boy" and "Challenging Casanova: Beyond the Stereotype of the Promiscuous Young Male."

"If you have a child or work with children you must read this book. Darrell takes us on a journey that is not only his story but the story of so many families and children today. Beautifully written, heartfelt and compelling it not only outlines the problems facing our children today including the tsunami of technology and pressure to "be a certain way"………but more importantly he gives us hope that through love and conscious parenting we can give our children what they really need.

Raised by Our Childhood Voices is full of beautiful stories about raising boys.

I hope this book becomes compulsory reading in schools around Australia and I thank Darrell for his wonderful contribution. His 2 sons are lucky to have him as their dad."

Dr Arne Rubinstein (mbbs, fracgp)
Author of "The Making of Men"

"In "**Raised by our Childhood Voices**," Darrell Brown is challenging us as parents to do right by our kids by first doing right by ourselves. "The greatest challenge of growing into a fully functioning adult comes from our ability to become aware of our unexamined childhood beliefs." His use of compelling stories not only hooks the reader, but models for us the ways we can teach our own kids without lecturing, and by finding the connection he urges us to seek."

Deborah Gilboa, MD,
Founder of Dr. G, Ask Doctor G;
Seen nationally on CBS Morning show, NBC, ABC and FOX

"**Raised by Our Childhood Voices,** by Darrell Brown, is a delightful read. However, this piece of work goes way beyond delightful and into the realm of the profound. If I said it is a historical novel in its presentation one might misunderstand, but only until reading.

It is the inner and outer exploration of one family's deep, personal, and emotionally honest history, explored through the eyes and heart of the boy, the man, the father, Darrell Brown. On a most essential level it is a sojourn into who we are, how we got to be this way, and how our choices in each moment not only affect our lives, and those we are closest to, but also future generations. I highly recommend this book for anyone, especially young parents. Now, everyone needs to go out and build a treehouse of their own!

Darrell you have told a really fine and important story here, and you have done it brilliantly. It deserves a really wide audience."

Patrick M. Houser,
Co-founder FathersToBe.org, educator and author,
Fathers To Be Handbook.

Darrell Brown has travelled a brave journey in search of being the best dad and person he can be. In "Raised by Our Childhood Voices", he shares that journey with both profound and in-the-moment experiences. The story of the tree house alone makes a wonderful read. Darrell has done the work required to transform the messages from his childhood into an understanding of what his children most need from him—the understanding, empathy and fun-loving dad he has become. His message to parents everywhere is to "listen for the voices that will get you to your next destination." These voices come from the most unexpected and often unwanted places, so the work is in learning to listen.

Bonnie Harris,
Author of "When Your Kids Push Your Buttons"
and "Confident Parents, Remarkable Kids: 8 Principles
for Raising Kids You'll Love to Live With."

"We need wisdom in this age and Darrell Brown delivers in Raised By Our Childhood Voices. You will read it in a day and be changed by it for a lifetime."

Dr. Lynne Kenney
Bloom: 50 things to say, think and do with anxious,
angry and over-the-top kids

"Raised by our Childhood Voices"

An inspirational read for any parent. Brown is a gripping storyteller. He generously shares his transformation journey from the wounds incurred in his upbringing that ultimately fuelled a commitment to learn how to do better as a father for his own boys and in the process healed himself. Brown pursues the answer to raising children from the far corners of the world and from a myriad of resources. He is truly a parent on a sacred pilgrimage and he serves up brilliant nuggets of insights, wisdom and perspective that leaves readers feeling they have not simply read a book, but rather that they have drank a calming balm for today's parenting angsts.

Alyson Schafer,
Family Therapist, Resident Parenting Expert for HuffPost Canada and best selling author of Breaking The Good Mom Myth, Honey, I Wrecked the Kids and Ain't Misbehavin'

"The journey of raising happy, confident, resilient children isn't always easy but I found Darrell's book an inspiring, compelling read as we all seemed to become part of his boys journey to adulthood too. The story about the tree house is a symbol of how the world needs more Dads like Darrell and it made me cry while Darrell's love for his boys sang out throughout this wonderfully gentle look at bringing up children. Boys need role models and Darrell is indeed a wonderful dad - what lucky boys they are! This book will inspire you to step back for a moment and look at how important your role as a parent is and it will gently lead you to become the best you can be."

Sue Atkins,
Author of 'Parenting Made Easy - How To Raise Happy Children. www.TheSueAtkins.com

www.ingramcontent.com/pod-product-compliance
Lightning Source LLC
Chambersburg PA
CBHW020611300426
44113CB00007B/604